My Life in the Sunshine

My Life in
the Sunshine

SEARCHING FOR MY FATHER
AND DISCOVERING MY FAMILY

NABIL AYERS

VIKING

VIKING
An imprint of Penguin Random House LLC
penguinrandomhouse.com

Portions of this book previously appeared on
The Root, Vox, The Stranger, and *Code Switch.*

Photograph on page v by Alan Braufman, used with permission.

LIBRARY OF CONGRESS CATALOGING-IN-PUBLICATION DATA
Names: Ayers, Nabil, author.
Title: My life in the sunshine: searching for my father and
discovering my family / Nabil Ayers.
Description: [1st.] | New York : Viking, 2022.
Identifiers: LCCN 2021045247 (print) | LCCN 2021045248 (ebook) |
ISBN 9780593295960 (hardcover) | ISBN 9780593295977 (ebook)
Subjects: LCSH: Ayers, Nabil. | Sound recording executives and
producers—United States—Biography. | Ayers, Nabil—Family. |
Ayers, Roy. | Fathers and sons. | LCGFT: Autobiographies.
Classification: LCC ML429.A97 A3 2022 (print) |
LCC ML429.A97 (ebook) | DDC 782.42164092 [B]—dc23
LC record available at https://lccn.loc.gov/2021045247
LC ebook record available at https://lccn.loc.gov/2021045248

Printed in the United States of America
1st Printing

DESIGNED BY MEIGHAN CAVANAUGH

To my parents,

Louise, Alan,

Shannon, and Jim

Contents

Straight Outta Compton

When I see a movie theater advertising *Straight Outta Compton*, I know how I'm about to spend the next two hours. *What better setting*, I think, *to watch a blockbuster about the LA rap group N.W.A. than this—the city from which it emerged.*

It is the summer of 2015, and I am in Los Angeles for the FYF music festival, where, backstage, I am repeatedly mistaken for a newly famous director who has made music videos for Kendrick Lamar, Kanye West, and Frank Ocean, and goes simply by his first name, Nabil. When I am introduced to some people, it's telling to hear their voices suddenly become more hip-hop—attempting to drop a bit of street into their words—an affectation they adopt only when they think they're meeting the rap video director.

"Not that Nabil" always elicits a humble apology. People aren't aware that even though he has made videos for hugely famous Black artists, Nabil is half-white and half-Iranian and looks much more white than I do.

While I was hoping to spend today at the festival with the artists I work with, instead I slowly walk around the newly revitalized downtown Los Angeles, recovering from a terrible case of food poisoning. The thought of seeing *Straight Outta Compton* in a comfortable, air-conditioned theater is much more appealing than the sensory overload of a crowded music festival. I force down the rest of my banana, guzzle my remaining seltzer, and still feeling weak, buy a ticket to the matinee.

Compton begins with a bang. In five fast minutes, the Los Angeles police destroy a drug house. Bullets and expletives fly, vicious dogs bark, and armored vehicles smash through residential walls like they're made of paper. And I'm completely sucked in, happy to have my mind numbed by Hollywood action, even if the portrayal is devastatingly true to life.

The bombastic opening scene ends, and the ensuing silence is broken by a piano sound, followed by an unmistakably familiar, lazy synthesizer melody. My pulse suddenly feels very present in my body. The song's patient, buoyant pace drives the camera's slow movement, which reveals a bedroom adorned with posters, records, DJ gear, and eventually a teenage boy lying down with his eyes closed and headphones wrapped around his head. The character, meant to be N.W.A. founder and producer Dr. Dre, wears a Los Angeles Dodgers jersey and hat as he subconsciously air-plays the piano, the congas, and the synthesizer along with the song. The overhead shot shows a record spinning with a legible red Polydor label at its center. The scene, which contains no dialogue, does everything to convey that Dre is lost in the music.

The camera closes in on Dre surrounded by album jackets, and I brace myself, knowing what I'm about to see.

And there it is, one album, standing apart with its white border. A man in a tight yellow T-shirt, a beard, and an Afro stands against a bright yellow background. His hand rests confidently on his hip, and he smiles as he looks off camera, radiating casual conviction. I can't read the album title, but I don't need to. I already know the man on the cover.

The music is so loud that I physically feel it in my chest and ass. The lyrics offer the first voices in the scene. "My life, my life, my life, my life . . . in the sunshine" blasts from the modern theater speakers and the chorus of male and female voices further shakes my weakened constitution.

I'm alone in a dark movie theater, three thousand miles from home, feeling skinny and sick and completely caught off guard by the most famous song by my father, Roy Ayers.

"Everybody Loves the Sunshine" was a moderate hit when it was first released in 1976. But it's grown over time—it's been sampled more than one hundred times by various artists including Mary J. Blige, Common, J. Cole, Tupac, Snoop Dogg, and Black Eyed Peas. It's been covered by D'Angelo and Cibo Matto, spanning decades and constantly refreshing itself into modern context. I've heard it in many different iterations over the years, a perennial, persistent reminder of my otherwise absent father.

After one very long minute of music, Dre's mother surprises

him by turning off the record, which snaps him out of his meditative state. My chest feels hot and my breath is short.

My first reaction is to sink into my cushy chair and look around the theater to see whether anyone is looking at me. *Is this what it would feel like to run into him?* I wonder. I'd last seen my father nine years earlier—when I was thirty-four—but that had been planned: a lunch in Seattle, my first ever meeting with him as an adult. The time before that, when I was eleven, I had no idea who he even was. Since moving back to New York City, where he lives, I'm always slightly, subconsciously on guard—ready to run into him. But I definitely wasn't expecting it in a dark movie theater in Los Angeles while getting over food poisoning.

Though my father and I live in the same city and are both in the music business, our paths have never crossed in the seven years that I've lived in New York. Occasionally, someone asks me how he's doing. It surprises me every time, and I usually respond with something like, "You'd probably know better than I would," which feels confrontational and often leads me to quickly offer a slightly apologetic, less biting explanation that he's never been a presence in my life.

How, I wonder, did a hippie child in New York City who never knew his father become a grown man who still didn't know his father but encountered his music regularly? Were moments like these truly coincidental? Or had my father's DNA guided me into a life in music, and ultimately to the places where his presence caught me off guard?

It has been over a year since I last tried to contact my father, and though I was unsuccessful, I decide it's time for another try. I know he won't become the father I'd never had, but maybe he can become the father I meet for lunch once or twice a year, the father who tells me about his life and my family history, the father who texts me each year on my birthday. He might not respond, but even if my father ignores me, I will have tried.

Little do I know in that moment that the impact of that minute in the theater—the intensity of hearing my father's music, my music, in a public place, through huge speakers and staring at his picture on a giant screen—will be the catalyst that opens up two centuries of perspective on my family.

My Life in the Sunshine

1.

Ubiquity

Dear, Louise—

Dance, swing, love, groove, and be as sweet as you are.

Roy

On a warm summer evening in 1970, Roy Ayers signed the glossy eight-by-ten photograph of himself and handed it to my mother with a proud smile. She felt awkward accepting an autographed photo from someone to whom she felt so close, but she also knew that beneath his tremendous talent and his infectious warmth, Roy was an ambitious, self-centered person who was steadfastly focused on his career, and unavailable to her.

Each time she saw him, she worried it might be the last.

My mother had first met Roy when she was twenty, in 1970, when she and her eighteen-year-old brother Alan—an aspiring jazz saxophonist who'd once met Roy—bumped into him one night at the Village Gate, a jazz club in New York City. By then, Roy Ayers was already quite well known. He had played alongside legendary musicians like Herbie Mann, Jack Wilson, and Leroy Vinnegar, and then, between 1967 and 1969, released three acclaimed albums under his own name on Atlantic Records. By 1970, Roy Ayers was a twenty-nine-year-old master of the vibraphone, a large, beautiful, complex instrument better known as the vibes.

That night at the Village Gate, my mother found Roy to be strikingly gorgeous with his beautiful brown eyes and his warm, confident smile. She also felt an instant chemistry. My mother has always been a talented conversationalist, and Roy matched her on that front with his charming and charismatic demeanor. When she also discovered that he didn't drink, smoke, or do drugs, and that he ate health food like she did, her fascination grew. She didn't have a phone at the time, so she couldn't give him her number. Instead, she just said, "Here's my address: 46-48 Downing Street in the Village. Knock on the door if you're ever in the neighborhood."

I've tried to create that night's scene in my mind: my tall, perfect-postured dancer mother looking just like the photographs I ingrained in my memory from those days, her wavy, golden-brown hair catching the dim light and her striking blue eyes turning heads in the smoke-filled club crowded with downtown hipsters; her brother Alan buzzing with excitement to see that night's performance, and elated to be chatting with a respected musician; and Roy, who I imagine looked like he did on his albums from around that time, with a tight Afro, and bushy sideburns. Roy was there only as a member of the audience that night, but I'm sure his energy lit up the room.

Anyone who wasn't lucky enough to talk to him that night likely wished that they were.

My mother remembers distinctly that when she met Roy, she said to herself, *This is the person I'm going to have a baby with.*

Looking back now, I can only imagine my mother felt pretty lost at the time. She and Alan were close, but she lived by herself in New York, and even though he visited often, Alan spent most of his time studying at the prestigious Berklee College of Music in Boston. My mother was a young woman in a gigantic city—a city she loved, but one in which she felt very alone. Roy represented a chance to create the family environment she'd never had growing up, along with the qualities she hoped for in her future child: kindness, artistry, and creativity.

But my mother went out with Roy only three times over the course of that year—not exactly a hot and heavy relationship, and definitely not one that would lead to a baby.

MY MOTHER AND ALAN grew up in Wantagh, Long Island, where their parents—Bert and Jean Braufman—bought their home for $9,000 in 1951. The brief stories my mother has told me about her childhood are heartbreaking: The loss of her younger sister Nancy, born with a mental disability and heart disease, who died at the age of seven. Her mother's multiple sclerosis, which was described to my adolescent mother as "an incurable disease." Her father's returning home from work, reeking of scotch and yelling so loudly that his voice made my mother's locked bedroom door vibrate. My mother's own battle with eating disorders during the twelve hard years she trained with Andre Eglevsky, one of the most respected ballet instructors in the world.

But weekends offered a glimpse of a different life when the family drove to New York City. On these trips my mother encountered movie-like views of bright lights and towering buildings, women with fabulous clothes and hairstyles, and people of different races who yelled, cursed, shoved, and haggled. I suspect it was these childhood trips that instilled in my mother her need to be in the city, among its diversity, creative energy, and volatility. When she was eighteen, she finally moved there.

In New York City, my mom was truly on her own—she wasn't a kid from the suburbs spending her parents' money on big nights on the town that ended in late-night taxi rides home. Instead, she earned $1.25 an hour waiting tables so she could afford the $125 per month rent for her apartment in Greenwich Village. The traditionally Italian neighborhood hosted a racially and economically diverse population that served as a daily reminder of my mother's draw to the city. She loved living there as much as Alan loved visiting.

Thanks to a former Long Island neighbor, my mother and Alan soon abandoned their secular Jewish upbringing and became members of the Baha'i Faith, a religion previously unfamiliar to them, but one whose ideals of peace and equality aligned with their own. Though the religion had emerged from the Middle East, the Baha'i Faith in New York in the early seventies attracted people of all races, from all walks of life. The Baha'i Faith opened up new possibilities for my mother and Alan. It connected them to like-minded people. And it ingrained them with deeper faith and spirituality.

When she wasn't waitressing at night or participating in Baha'i gatherings, my mother spent her days exploring New York City's endless neighborhoods. On these long walks, she'd often stop to watch children play in the parks. It was those moments that ignited her choice to become a young, single mother. She wasn't focused on a relationship—that could come later in life. But while she was young, she wanted a friend to love who would love her back, someone she could shower with attention and who would never feel as lonely or upset as she did growing up, someone to balance out the trauma of her own childhood. Though my mother wasn't actively looking for the father of her imaginary companion, the moment she met Roy, she believed she'd found him, which made her even more determined to connect with him.

ON APRIL 27, 1971, after leaving an event at the Baha'i Center, my mother insisted to Alan that they visit Roy's nearby apartment.

She wanted to try to get pregnant that night.

It had been several months since my mother had seen Roy—so

long that she worried that he wouldn't remember her, or that he might be with another woman when they arrived. But when Roy opened the door, he welcomed them both with long hugs. They spent the evening catching up in his sparsely furnished living room, discussing their lives in New York City, and music—Alan had joined Roy onstage to perform a Miles Davis song a few months earlier. Then the power went out.

Suspecting that the blackout wasn't citywide, Roy had a car take them to my mother's apartment. There they continued to talk, but my mother's desire to get pregnant was at the forefront of her thoughts. When Alan fell asleep on the couch, my mother and Roy retired to the makeshift bedroom—separated by thick, homemade curtains—where she slept on a mattress on the living room floor.

There, my mother bluntly told Roy she really wanted to get pregnant with him. He agreed, but he also made it clear that if she did get pregnant, she'd be on her own. Roy had always been up front with my mother—his career was on the rise, and he had no interest in a serious relationship. But my mother desperately wanted a baby with him, and this was her chance.

My mother's memory has always astonished me. To this day, she can describe the percussive guitar strum that her neighbor— the folk singer Richie Havens—played in his impromptu apartment performances, and the way the sound traveled up the stairs to her apartment; she can recount with tactile detail the material with which she sewed the dress she wore on the night she met Roy; and she can describe the thick curtains—cut from a gigantic Indian bedspread—that separated her and Roy from Alan on the night I was conceived. But no amount of prodding gleaned any more information about her conversation with Roy on that night, the conversation that led to me. My mother insists that it was that brief—that easy.

Likewise, Alan's memories are not only consistent with my mother's, they're easily outweighed by his simple justification of the circumstances: "It was New York City in the early seventies."

SEVERAL WEEKS LATER my mother started to experience the nausea and dizziness that confirmed what she already knew: That night with Roy had worked. She'd gotten pregnant.

When she was sixteen weeks along, my mother called Roy to tell him. It was a call she made out of courtesy more than anything else. Sure, there was a part of her that hoped he'd say, "I love you, let's raise our child together." But she also knew that wasn't realistic. And although that fantasy clouded her thinking, deep down, my mother knew that her own two-parent childhood—though perfect on paper, with a brother and a house in the suburbs—had been far from perfect in real life. She knew that she could do a better job raising a child on her own.

Roy reacted to the news with detachment, saying things like, "I'm so happy for you. That's great. That's what you wanted." His response confirmed what my mother had expected and what they'd agreed upon: she would raise me on her own. There was no attempt by either of them to share me—my mother viewed a part-time father as far worse than no father at all.

Despite the response being exactly what she expected—exactly what Roy had agreed to the night they slept together—my mother was still in tears after the call. She felt rejected, and she had difficulty reconciling that feeling with the reality she knew she had intentionally created.

Later that night, though, my mother talked to Alan. He vowed to be present in my life. He assured her that she was going to have a happy, healthy baby, and that they'd figure everything out. My mother had no money, but she was resourceful. She had Alan's emotional support, and more than anything, she was committed to being a good mother. After Alan calmed her down, my mother felt a deep sense of relief that she didn't have to share her baby with anyone.

She didn't see Roy for the rest of the pregnancy.

People have asked my mother how it felt that my father left her. And her response was always that he didn't leave her. She intentionally picked someone who was married to his career and was completely unavailable. She describes her pregnancy as something remarkably positive, something that happened because of love.

People have also asked me how I feel about my mother's decision to have me knowing that my father wouldn't be involved. Her decision was unquestionably selfish—one that would shape my entire life. But for a long time, rather than admitting that to anyone who asked, I focused on the positives. My mother took a huge risk, hoping that Roy's best qualities—his kindness, his talent, and his magnetism—would transfer to me, and that I wouldn't inherit or experience what she saw as his worst qualities: his unreliability and his self-centeredness. But she never concerned herself with the variables that she couldn't control. Instead, my mother set out to give me a wonderful childhood, raising me in safe, supportive environments, and challenging the traditional definition of family.

And for a long time, that was good enough for me. Until it wasn't.

DURING MY MOTHER'S PREGNANCY, Alan took a semester off to be with her in New York. When she was eight months along, he gave her a copy of the book *The Dawn-Breakers: Nabíl's Narrative of the Early Days of the Bahá'í Revelation*. Nabil was a Baha'i historian who documented the persecution of the Baha'is during the religion's formative years. Alan—impressed with the writer's story and deeply invested in the Baha'i Faith—suggested to my mother that she name me Nabil if I was a boy. They both loved the way it sounded, and even more, they loved the name's meaning: noble, learned, and generous.

So when I was born, on a winter day in 1972, that was the name I was given. Nabil.

My middle name comes from more pedestrian origins. My mother had seen the opera *Amahl and the Night Visitors* on TV right before I was born, and she loved how nice the son was to his mother.

Hence my middle name. Amahl.

My last name, though, was never a topic of discussion until

years later, when I began to establish myself in the music world. I would be my mother's child: Nabil Amahl Braufman.

IN 1970, ROY AYERS RELEASED the album *Ubiquity*. An inscription on the album's back cover explains the title:

One of us could be somewhere. Some of us could be elsewhere. All of us could be everywhere. UBIQUITY is being somewhere, elsewhere and everywhere—always.

By design, my father was never part of our lives. But he's always existed in my life—somewhere, elsewhere, and everywhere. Always.

2.

Valley of Search

From a very young age, I felt a deep, emotional connection with music. As far back as I can remember, certain tones and chord changes could affect and sometimes startle me. The feelings were physical—like light kicks in the stomach that I knew wouldn't hurt. In fact, my earliest childhood memories are musical: playing worn-out John Coltrane records with my mother and Alan on a delicate wooden turntable. Listening to Alan practice his saxophone for several hours each day, establishing in my head melodies that would later become songs of his. And, of course, playing my drums.

When I was five months old, we moved to Cambridge, Massachusetts, to be near Alan, who was now back in school. After two years working at Harvard's Widener Library, my mother enrolled at nearby Bunker Hill Community College to earn an associate's degree.

Though I barely remember the five years my mother and I spent living in Cambridge, certain formative moments stand out. Alan may have given me my most defining characteristic—my name—but only a couple of years later, when I was two and a half, he gave me something else that's been equally important to my identity: a beat-up but very real orange-and-silver-splotched Ludwig drum set.

I have an image of my uncle Alan, young and scrawny, his midseventies bushy mustache perfectly matching his wavy pile of black hair, smiling proudly as he brought each piece of the drum set down the stairs to our basement apartment. Each drum was large, bright, and shiny with a glossy, wrapped finish.

The first sound I heard—the metal on metal of the cymbals hitting one another—was shockingly loud, causing me to flinch. It took seemingly forever for the noise to fade: the high-pitched metal sizzle foreshadowing how tinnitus would sound thirty years later.

From that day onward, I carried around my drumsticks everywhere we went. I wanted people to know who I was and what I did. Sometimes I carried one lone cymbal—a weighty, sharp, metallic accessory that had no place in a child's hands. When I accidentally dropped it on my big toe and a pool of blood stained the cement under my bare foot, I realized that I really only needed a pair of sticks to announce my identity: I am a *drummer*.

. . .

IN CAMBRIDGE, MY MOTHER'S JOB at Widener Library allowed me to attend the elite preschool on the Harvard campus.
My mother loves to joke that while she attended Bunker Hill
Community College, I attended Harvard. But this is sort of an
allegory for what was happening at the time: my mother was set
on raising our standard of living—more for my benefit than for
her own, even though she was only twenty-five. Yet she never
gave me inspiring childhood lectures in which she told me that I
could do anything or be anyone I wanted. Those lessons were
reserved for children for whom success *wasn't* a given. My mother
knew I'd be successful from day one, and she doubled down on
her prediction by surrounding us with great people: my schoolteachers, Alan, our friends, our neighbors, and in particular the
Baha'i community.

While in Cambridge, we attended monthly Baha'i feasts. Baha'is
don't drink, so I was never the kid who watched the adult party
grow louder and devolve into sloppy arguments over who was
okay to drive. Baha'i feasts ended as peacefully as they began.

I remember one winter feast we hosted, our small apartment
was so packed that the overflow of coats was stacked up in our
bathtub. For a three-year-old, it was the perfect place to hide,
and I buried myself in a cozy pile of wool and tweed. When the
party began to wind down, I heard my mother searching for me,
her voice growing more worried as she called out my name, her
powerful dancer footsteps hitting the wood floor. When she

finally walked into the bathroom, I was struck by her look of concern and quickly straightened my smile, readying to apologize. But then she cracked a smile, and we both burst into laughter. My mother was learning how to be a single mother one day at a time, and when the party ended, yes, we were alone again, but we were together.

AFTER GRADUATING FROM BERKLEE, Alan moved back to New York City. My mother and I stayed in Cambridge, but throughout my childhood, no matter where we were living, I always spent at least a few months of each year at Alan's apartment at 501 Canal Street.

In the seventies, New York was an infamously dangerous, desperate city on the brink of bankruptcy. No matter the neighborhood, there were specific blocks to avoid because of muggers, drug dealers, and gangs. But as dingy and desolate as it was, the area around 501 Canal never felt unsafe to me. It was a quiet haven—an underdeveloped zone of the city that went unnoticed until it boomed two decades later as Tribeca.

Gene Ashton, my godfather—a pianist and multi-instrumentalist who performs as Cooper-Moore—found the run-down, four-story building on the far west side of the downtown strip known for its abundant junk stores and discount electronics shops. He persuaded Alan and some fellow Boston colleagues to move to New York City and join him there.

The total rent for 501 Canal was $550 per month, which allowed its occupants to work very little and focus on playing music. But to clarify, 501 Canal was not a high-ceilinged fortress or a trendy, industrial, metal-and-concrete compound. It was an off-the-grid, prickly splinter of a building that honestly should have been condemned years before.

Opening the door was like entering a haunted house. Even at night, it took time to adjust to the extreme darkness of the space, which was lit by a single fatigued, yellowing bulb that hung high above the stairs.

Inside, the air felt cold and smelled of dry wood and dust, thanks to the building's being unoccupied for the previous twenty years. A steep wooden staircase visibly slouched to the left, almost floating, barely attached to the wall that somehow supported it. Every step whined and complained under human feet. Even as a child, I contemplated whether I'd be better off running up or down when the stairs finally collapsed under me.

The building had no heat, so during the winter, Alan sealed his windows with large sheets of opaque plastic that puffed inward like dirty balloons. On the coldest nights, liquids froze solid if we forgot to put them in the fridge, which was warmer than any room.

But when you added in the tenants, 501 Canal became more than just a dilapidated building—it was a multiracial epicenter of jazz. In the barely habitable attic lived the drummer Jimmy Hopps, who played with heavy hitters like Roland Kirk, Charles Tolliver, and Pharoah Sanders. The bassist Chris Amberger lived on the fourth floor. Below him was Gene. My uncle Alan lived on the second floor with one roommate, David S. Ware, the acclaimed saxophonist who went on to play with Cecil Taylor and make many celebrated records of his own. The drummer Tom Bruno occupied the street-level storefront space.

Many New York jazz venues refused to book the emerging crop of young, nontraditional musicians, so in 1974, the group began to use 501 Canal's storefront as a performance space. While the space didn't have a name, it quickly became a key part of New York's downtown loft jazz scene, known for its Friday night concerts, and had an enduring influence on jazz and downtown culture.

AT 501 CANAL, my uncle Alan developed a strong, recognizable tone to his own playing—one I can vividly hear in my head—which belies his soft-spoken, kind demeanor. For Alan, "a quick practice" meant two hours of playing at full volume—not scales or exercises—but intense, melodic runs with notes so strong they resonated in the apartment's loose floorboards. If you heard Alan play then, you'd assume he had a beast of a personality. But if you met him on the street, you'd never guess someone so mellow could harness such fierceness. To this day, Alan remains a calm and unassuming secret powerhouse.

During my childhood visits to 501 Canal, Alan and I often played music together in the performance space. Recordings of us from those days reveal a bossy but not rhythmless child drummer and an unbelievably patient saxophonist who considered our sessions part of his several-hours-per-day practice regimen.

In early 1975, Alan released his debut album, *Valley of Search*, a free jazz offering that embodies the grit and chaos of New

York City in the midseventies. Listening to *Valley of Search* now brings me back to an exciting, often intimidating city overflowing with creative energy. But while the feelings I associate with *Valley of Search* are uniquely New York, the sounds are distinctly 501 Canal. At once dissonant and beautiful, spare yet cacophonous, *Valley of Search* inhales and exhales the chaos of a gigantic populace.

The album's title is taken from an 1860 writing by the Baha'i Faith founder Bahá'u'lláh. The Valley of Search is the first of seven valleys in the writing, in which the seeker must cleanse his heart and follow his own path.

As a three-year-old, I didn't comprehend the concepts embedded in my uncle's album. But I felt them, and they became part of me. The album's title, its striking cover art—mostly black with a bird and the sun watching over line-drawn mountains and a valley—and the heaviness of the music were part of my upbringing, a tactile, audible lesson in spirituality.

And of course, there was the song he named after me.

"Little Nabil's March" is an unrelenting stomp of drums, tambourines, and whistles under a joyous, celebratory melody. It's a song that Alan and I played together regularly before he recorded it, and Alan's melody always inspired me to romp. It was the drumming equivalent of a child jumping up and down with excitement.

3.

A Love Supreme

In historian Richard Rothstein's book *The Color of Law: A Forgotten History of How Our Government Segregated America*, he outlines in great detail the many deliberate policies that kept America's housing projects and entire neighborhoods segregated well into the seventies—something that should have been remedied a hundred years earlier, during Reconstruction. Rothstein asserts that, had we taken more steps to integrate housing, we would be living in a drastically different, healthier, more accepting country.

North Village Apartments in Amherst, Massachusetts, the university family housing development where my mother and I moved in the summer of 1977, when I was five, was living proof of Rothstein's claim.

While my mother finished her college degree and earned her MBA at UMass, we lived in a rent-subsidized apartment that cost forty-five dollars a month. We survived through welfare, food stamps, and potlucks within our community of international families. I had no idea we were poor, because our quality of life was excellent, and I knew very few people who had more than we did.

During the day, hundreds of children of every ethnic origin and mixture ran free over grassy landscaped hills and through communal backyards. We rode bikes and roller-skated without helmets. We taught each other words and phrases in different languages and never made fun of anyone's accent.

At the time of my birth, mixed-race marriage had been legal in the United States for only five years. But in Amherst, many of my friends were also of mixed race. Cultural differences existed— no two homes smelled of the same spices—but the fact that we were all different somehow made us all the same. We were sheltered from the rest of America.

While few of us lived with or even knew both of our parents, none of us was the weird kid because of it. One friend's mother had fled her abusive husband to live in our sanctuary. Another neighbor's father was in prison. In our neighborhood, mothers were strong and fathers were scarce—mythical, like unicorns: occasionally talked about, although few of us could claim to have actually known one.

. . .

THE YEAR I TURNED SEVEN, my mother asked me what I wanted for my birthday. I answered quickly: a party and a chocolate cake. I'd had a birthday party every year, but I'd never had a junk food cake.

When the day arrived, a dozen of us crowded into our small kitchen. Everyone joined in to sing "Happy Birthday," a chorus of kids rushing the song. A brown cake somehow magically appeared on our Formica table, festive flames wavering atop each of its colorful candles. My eyes widened as I inhaled, and after one strong puff on the candles, the kids around me began to cheer.

I jammed my fork into the shiny brown triangle on my plate, excited, but the first bite was dry, crumbly, and disappointingly familiar—not exotic and gooey like I imagined a chocolate cake would taste.

Each of my friends was making an expression similar to what I imagined my own face looked like, but my mother was smiling proudly. Finally, one honest guest spoke up, bluntly articulating what we were all thinking: "This isn't chocolate."

It turns out my mother had actually baked a *carob* cake, without sugar or eggs, thinking the roomful of children wouldn't know the difference between real chocolate and its distant, more healthy brown cousin, carob.

For my next birthday, I guilted my mother into buying a *real* ice cream cake from Baskin-Robbins, which was custom decorated—

with colors that resembled no real food—to look like the face of the drummer in the band Kiss. I savored every bite, eating faster when I realized the drummer's face might melt.

OVER THE YEARS when I tell stories like these, I'm often met with a sympathetic reaction, as if I'd just illustrated the deprivation of my childhood. But to me, my childhood was perfect. Of course, there were toys and amusement park trips I couldn't have. But my childhood wasn't about what I couldn't have, it was about what I had: a community of wonderful people among whom I felt supported and encouraged, loved, and accepted. In my world, "real families" existed only on our tiny black-and-white TV, and even those had static running through them.

In particular, I had my mother, with whom I spent a lot of time. We didn't own a car, but it was easy to find a ride or take the free bus to the Mountain Farms Mall, where I insisted on seeing the movie *Grease* seven separate times. We'd wander around Amherst's historic center of town and buy a used record if we could afford it. On special occasions, we'd share one appetizer at a fancy restaurant. My mother brought me along to everything, from her dry business classes at UMass to her weekly African dance classes, which pulsed with the energy of two live drummers.

She was also extremely supportive of my growing interest in drumming. In North Village, I spent hours each day playing drums, listening to music, and often combining the two by playing along with records, which required me to push our small stereo to sizzling levels of distortion in order to be heard while I played. The walls between apartments were so thin that we could sometimes hear voices from next door, especially during an argument, which caused me to cringe silently—or an uproarious laugh, which I always joined in on. Once, our neighbor Doug complained about the noise from my practicing, and my mother sternly told him, "Go fuck yourself!" before slamming the door in his face. Then she turned to me, her finger pointing toward my bedroom. "Go play your drums," she said calmly, as if telling me to do my homework.

Thanks to my mother's constant presence, I never thought of myself as lacking a father. During the rare times I fought with her, I never said anything that began with "If you hadn't decided to raise me without a father . . ." And she never considered a blow like "If there was a man in the house . . ." We heard other mothers complain about missing fathers, but that sentiment never occurred to us because my father wasn't missing. My mother's steadfast determination to take on all responsibility without placing blame on my father rubbed off on me and it stayed with me. I didn't envy my friends with siblings and fathers: I could run around with them all day and eat dinner in their homes at night. And then I could come home, listen to or watch whatever I wanted, and have all of my mother's attention.

WHEN I WAS SEVEN, Michael and his mother moved in a few doors down from us in North Village. Michael and I quickly became friends and he introduced me to *The Dukes of Hazzard*, a TV show about two wild Southern boys who drove a car with a gigantic Confederate flag on its roof and a horn that blasted the Confederate anthem "I Wish I Was in Dixie."

Michael was white, and though he had no issue with me or any of the other children of color, I once heard him reciting a poem that began "Forty damn niggers came knockin' at my door. Whippin' my ass up and down the floor."

I knew that racism existed. Alex Haley's *Roots* TV miniseries had aired in 1977 and had shone a new light on slavery and racism in America. But I'd never experienced racism firsthand or heard anyone use a racist word or phrase.

I was confused by Michael's poem. But not threatened. He certainly wasn't calling me a name, and I understood that. It sounded as if he were simply repeating something he'd heard.

"You shouldn't say that word," I instructed.

"What word?"

I explained that "nigger" was a bad word for Black people. But I wasn't upset because he'd offended *me*, I was upset because he'd used an offensive term. I knew my father was Black, and I knew that some people saw me as Black. But at my young age— in our idyllic community—I hadn't ever had to confront a situation like this.

I asked Michael to change the word to something else that worked rhythmically: assholes, fuckers . . . just nothing derogatory.

He agreed and it never came up again.

. . .

MICHAEL WASN'T MY ONLY FRIEND in North Village. The day my mother and I moved in, we met our neighbor Diane, whose son Tony was three years younger than me and shared my birthday. Like us, Diane was white and Tony's Black father wasn't in the picture. Tony and I easily passed for brothers, and the four of us soon became a makeshift family. On summer afternoons, we rode in the back seat of Diane's car, laughing as our ice cream dripped out of our cones and down our arms onto the hot pleather seat. We'd travel home from the grocery store or the swimming pool, the wide-open car windows creating a warm vacuum that pushed and pulled our Afros sideways.

Looking back at photographs of the four of us during that time in our lives, I see two white moms and their young, Blackish sons who'd never known their fathers. Tony and I were wearing homemade or handed-down clothing, and our Afros were both lumpy and home-cut. Our mothers squinted in the sunlight, wearing era-defining short shorts and large, round glasses.

There isn't a hint of *This is a hard life but we are making it*. It's quite the opposite. The photographs say, *This is a wonderful life and we've made it. And it's only going to get better.*

4.

Destroyer

As far back as I can remember, I've wanted to be in a band. But even at a young age, as a racially mixed kid, I didn't identify with most of the musicians I saw or listened to. I was exposed to a good balance of Black and white artists, but I didn't look like anyone whose picture appeared on the albums we owned. The Beatles had pale skin and straight, brown hair that I knew I wasn't capable of growing. Stevie Wonder was a much darker shade of brown than I was, and his Afro was tighter than mine. I knew I was somewhere in between these people, with no one to directly emulate.

I couldn't change who I was, nor did I want to, but finally, I found something attainable in the band Kiss. I had no idea what they looked like in real life, and for that reason, I felt there was nothing that stopped me from looking like them.

The first record I ever bought was Kiss's *Destroyer*. I was five at the time. I remember racing down the seemingly towering aisle of the UMass Amherst bookstore as my mother stood back, admiring my alphabet skills, until I found it, right above the K section: a giant twelve-inch-by-twelve-inch square with four one-dimensional characters clustered atop the rubble of a bombed-out city.

At home, I played the record over and over. I studied every inch of the record's colorful jacket, memorizing details like the fan club's New York City mailing address. I read the tiny text on the record's circular label, which featured the word "Casablanca" in neon-like letters—the same label I later saw on my Village People record.

Two years later, when I was seven, my mother took me to see Kiss at Madison Square Garden. I'd seen lots of live music as a child, but seeing Kiss was a life-changing experience that contradicted the intimacy of the jazz I'd known at 501 Canal with the bombast and spectacle of arena rock.

I remember the sunlike intensity of the giant, lit-up *KISS* letters on the stage caused me to look away, even though I didn't want to. And when I blinked, the letters remained burned into the insides of my eyelids. I can still recall the musty smell and taste of twenty thousand people—the smoke and the sweat—on that muggy night. The volume of the band was sometimes dwarfed by that of the crowd, and my chest rumbled. I felt simultaneously overwhelmed, frightened, and ecstatic. More than anything else that night, though,

I focused on the drummer Peter Criss, feeling more strongly than ever that I wanted to do what he did.

Later that year for Halloween, I went as Peter. My official Kiss costume, purchased at the drugstore with saved-up allowance money, was an abrasive mask that smelled of toxic paint and displayed a stark white face with black whiskers protruding from its cheeks.

After that Halloween, my mother and I thought we could do better. We removed the mattress from my wooden bed frame and replaced it with my drum set, converting the frame into a drum riser. To complete my transformation, my mother painted my face like Peter's. After she applied a layer of white face paint, I was unable to form any facial expression, my pores sealed with thick, white goop. *How do they do this every night?* I wondered as my mother carefully applied my green-and-black eye makeup. When she finished my red lips, I put on my Kiss T-shirt, sat at my drums, and blasted *Destroyer*.

"You look just like Peter Criss!" my mother exclaimed proudly.

WHEN I WAS SEVEN, I inherited a used pogo stick. I got so good at it that one afternoon I counted two thousand jumps without stopping. As I jumped, a small crowd amassed and someone called the *Amherst Record*, which quickly dispatched a photographer to cover the important event.

IT'S A RECORD FOR HIM, ANYWAY, read the next day's front-page headline, above a picture of me wearing a New York Yankees T-shirt tucked into gym shorts, proudly jumping on my pogo stick. Now I think it must have been a slow news day. But back then, I felt famous. Kids, parents, and even strangers saw me and yelled things like "Nice job!" and "There he is!"

The recognition gave me a newfound buzz of unfamiliar energy, an extra spring in my step. I'd had my first dose of fame and the unique rush that comes from getting attention simply for doing something you like to do.

I loved it. And I hoped that someday I could get that same feeling from playing drums.

IN THIRD GRADE, my friends Eduardo and Tabish and I decided we needed to start a band because we listened to the same music. By this time, I had graduated from Kiss because their disco-infused album *Dynasty* turned me off (Eduardo and Tabish felt similarly). But we each responded in the same visceral way to the exciting new sounds on our radios from new wave bands such as Blondie and the Knack.

Eduardo was a stocky kid whose round face was nearly the same color as his sandy bob haircut, which had lighter streaks running through it. He owned a real electric guitar. Tabish was the outgoing youngest member of a large Pakistani family, and his instrument required significantly less investment and skill than mine or Eduardo's: he played a pair of thick, eight-inch-long wooden sticks.

I, of course, was on drums.

At one point, I had tried out Eduardo's guitar and experienced the true frustration of a novice. Drums can be hard at first, but if you stomp on a bass drum pedal, it sounds like a bass drum. If you hit a cymbal, it sounds like a cymbal. Guitar is totally different. That day, my left hand and wrist began to cramp as they attempted to grapple with the guitar's neck. The strings felt sharper, harder, and more metallic than I'd ever imagined. I didn't yet have the life experience to understand why it wasn't easy to play guitar, but I remember thinking, as my heart thumped, *Wow, I'd really like to learn how to play this instrument, but for now, I'm glad I'm the drummer in our band.*

One day after practice, we decided we needed to book a show. We weren't thinking about girls or money. We were just thinking about playing music . . . which we couldn't actually play as a group. We didn't have a singer either. But when we got good enough at playing along with "Macho Man" by the Village People and "One Way or Another" by Blondie, we decided our two-song set was ready.

I'd seen a lot of live music for a seven-year-old, and with all of that experience, I was ready to promote my own band's upcoming show. I drew a flyer to put up at the laundromat—the hub of information in North Village. It was functional if rudimentary, with the date, time, location, and one-dollar admission charge clearly presented, along with our band's name: Nightmare. Above the name was the headline: ROCK CONCERT!

The show was scheduled to take place in our living room on a Saturday afternoon. Tabish, Eduardo, and I had practiced our two songs and earned the uncompromising support of my mother and the other parents, but we didn't know how different it would feel playing in front of an audience.

That afternoon, about twenty people packed the room and occupied our couch, chairs, and floor, and we played with our backs to the windows, thick curtains blocking out the light. The songs sounded nothing like they did at practice. Tabish, Eduardo, and I faced the audience, not each other, making it impossible for us to recognize as a unit when musical changes approached. I felt like I was playing alone.

Despite the fact that I suspected we weren't very good and that we had let everyone in for free, several people—all of whom we knew—left us dollar bills or change and told us nice things on the way out. After the concert, we sat on the floor facing each other as we counted and split the door money, which was just under ten dollars.

Though I didn't realize it at the time, something very momentous had happened that day: I'd formed a band, practiced, and promoted and played a show. In return, I'd earned two precious things: money and attention. It was my first introduction to the music business.

5.

Ascension

When I was seven, I got to go backstage at a concert for the first time. The show was at the UMass football stadium, which was just one mile from where my mother and I lived. I distinctly remember the gray cement hallways felt cold and futuristic as we worked our way through a cast of fast-moving, colorful characters. The people carried the familiar and universal energy of music that I'd already sensed at concerts in New York and Cambridge. But actually being behind the scenes was more intimate. Important-looking men and women spoke into walkie-talkies. Others traversed the hallways carrying guitars and water coolers. I knew that all of these tasks—no matter how mundane—were part of a bigger picture, and I was fascinated by even the most minor detail.

During the concert, my mother and I watched from the loosely crowded photographers' pit—close to the gigantic stage—and I tried to make sense of everyone's role, from the musicians to the techs, who crouched as they scurried around. The afternoon audience seemed more interested in the scene than the music.

That all changed when the person we'd come to see walked onstage. Roy Ayers had arrived.

Roy's song "Everybody Loves the Sunshine" was just three years old at the time. Though it wasn't the first time I'd heard the song—we owned the album—it's the first time I recall feeling connected to it. And it's the first time I'd heard it performed live, outside, in the afternoon sunshine. As the lazy chords drifted over the audience, I remember feeling a gentle breeze on my arm and smelling what I already knew was marijuana smoke from the slow-swaying bodies around me.

We owned a few of Roy's records, and I knew that he was my father. My mother and I had run into him a few times in New York when I was too young to remember. But this was the first time I'd seen him perform, and as much as I was taken by his music, I was drawn to his personality. I could tell that he was a star through the way he smiled, the way he pointed or nodded to acknowledge individual people in the crowd and the enthusiastic way they responded, and the way in which he interacted with his band. When he was onstage, the entire stadium belonged to him.

My mother and I left the concert after Roy's set. Later that afternoon, I was in our communal backyard, building a rock concert out of Legos on the grass while my mother read quietly in a flimsy plastic lounge chair. Our soundtrack was the muted thump and indiscernible notes of the concert still happening in the distance. The band—which I'd heard of and had presumed to be a hard rock band due to their name and skeleton logo—was the Grateful Dead.

But it was the laid-back groove of "Everybody Loves the Sunshine" that still dominated my body as I assembled my Legos. It was the perfect soundtrack to the breezy spring afternoon and the smell of fresh-cut grass. The lyrics "My life, my life, my life, my life . . . in the sunshine" repeated in my head.

For a long time, the backstage pass from that concert lived in our photo album. The palm-sized manila peel-off rectangle smelled like medical tape and read in bold green letters:

U-MASS SPRING CONCERT
MAY 12, 1979
THE GRATEFUL DEAD
PATTI SMITH
ROY AYERS
ACCESS TO ALL AREAS

Handwritten on the pass in blue ink, in the penmanship of a seven-year-old, are three words: "BOO!" next to THE GRATEFUL DEAD. "BOO!" next to PATTI SMITH. "YAY!" next to ROY AYERS.

Years later, when I was well into my teens, I found out that my mother and I had arrived at the stadium early that day, that she had talked our way backstage by telling the bouncer that I was Roy's son, and that we actually met with him. According to my mother, during that surprise drop-in, she dominated the conversation with a flash update on my seven years of life, bragging about how I walked at an early age and was one grade ahead in school, and about my drumming. She said that Roy was exuberant in our exchange, receptive and even somewhat inquisitive, as if catching up after just a few months apart during an otherwise normal life.

I don't remember this encounter with my father. I only remember the sound of his music, and the way he drew all the sunshine toward him that day.

6.

Electric Ladyland

During our four years in Amherst, I continued to spend chunks of time in New York City with my uncle Alan. Sometimes we got a ride with someone from Amherst—it was as simple as my mother and me overhearing someone in the laundromat talking about driving to New York City that weekend and my mother asking for a ride. When we didn't have a ride, we took the Peter Pan bus, a four-hour trip that offered the constant reminder—through the smell of old piss—that it had a bathroom.

By that time, Alan had taken up aikido and had earned his black belt. He sometimes took two classes a day at New York Aikikai, the dojo that sat on the second floor above an auto shop on West Eighteenth Street. I frequently watched Alan's aikido classes, where I'd draw pictures of drums or New York City skyscrapers with crayons in the corner of the room. My focus was interrupted every time a sweaty adult body slammed down on the mat three feet in front of me.

Aikido offered another window into Alan's spirituality. Even though people were quite literally being thrown across the room, attacked with large wooden sticks, and yelled at in sharp, arresting tones, I knew that what I witnessed wasn't violent. It was the opposite. Aikido was an intense, powerful art form—like ballet or tai chi, but with more physical contact.

To me, my mother and Alan were just two people in their twenties getting by in New York City and Amherst. But looking back, all these elements fit together—ballet, jazz, the Baha'i Faith, aikido—as pieces of a quest for greater understanding of, and participation in, the world. And a quest for greater spirituality.

ALAN'S AIKIDO CLASSES WERE HELD around the corner from Roy's apartment, and he occasionally ran into Roy. On one of those afternoons, in 1980, when I was eight, Roy invited Alan to bring me to visit him in the recording studio.

Growing up, even though I knew I'd met my father a few times, like during the concert at UMass one year earlier, I didn't remember all of those moments. All I had to go on was my mother's recollections. In her telling, the emphasis was never on how great my father was, rather it was about how happy she was to show me off to him and how she introduced me: *Nabil Amahl Braufman.* She'd say those three words proudly, as if presenting a prince or an award.

Unlike the UMass concert, where I remembered his music but not him, that evening at Electric Lady recording studios in Greenwich Village, New York City, is the first time I actually remember meeting my father.

I didn't realize how legendary Electric Lady was: Jimi Hendrix had named his album *Electric Ladyland* after the studio, which had been built for him in 1970. Everyone from Sly and the Family Stone to David Bowie had recorded there. It was also the place where Kiss had recorded their incredible album *Destroyer*.

Roy was at the height of his success during this time, and for his new album, he'd returned to Electric Lady, where he'd recorded some of *Everybody Loves the Sunshine* a few years earlier (a framed, autographed album cover remains on the studio's wall to this day).

I'd imagined Electric Lady to be a tall building with musicians playing visibly in brightly lit, gigantic windows. But it was the opposite: a secret space hiding in plain sight on Eighth Street just off Sixth Avenue, thousands of people walking and driving by every day, many of them unknowingly listening to music that was recorded inside its walls.

"It's Alan . . . and Nabil. Here to see Roy." Alan's sincere, nonthreatening tone caused Electric Lady's cold metal door to buzz open. We were greeted by a man who was likely used to a twenty-four-hour parade of rock stars, drug dealers, and intense fans. When he saw a mellow guy and a kid, he had no trouble letting us in.

My breath quickened as we walked down a short, surprisingly silent hallway. But I wasn't thinking about meeting my father. I was thinking about Kiss and the fact that I was somehow inside the building where they'd recorded. I wondered whether they were in the building right then, and if so—were they wearing makeup?

A thick, padded door opened, revealing a studio lounge, with several people sitting on couches. Bright, colorful music-related art and gold record award plaques covered the walls, reassuring me that this was a place where magic was made.

Alan introduced us to the room, where we were greeted with the sight of perfectly round Afros, painstakingly long dreadlocks, and genuine smiles. I heard phrases like "What's happenin'?" and "All right, man."

I could see my reflection in a large window that took up an entire wall. Behind the glass stood my father, Roy. His hands cupped both sides of an oversized pair of studio headphones. His eyes were closed, unable to see the large, scientific-looking microphone directly in front of him. His face smiled as his mouth moved, but I didn't hear anything.

I stood silently, internally buzzing with the excitement of my surroundings. I made eye contact with a woman who smiled at me, and I wanted to talk to her, but I didn't know what to say. I wondered whether she knew who I was. If she'd asked, I wouldn't have said, "Roy is my father." I would have said, "I know Roy."

I knew the difference. If I'd thought of Roy as my father, I would have been excited to see him. I would have thought, as I waited, about what I wanted to tell him about my life: That third grade really wasn't much harder than second. That I loved Amherst, and I also loved spending so much time in New York. That

I was proud of my mother, who was almost finished with her MBA, and that we were planning to move back to New York once she graduated. That I played drums every day.

But I didn't think of him as my father. Sure, I knew some basic information about him: I knew he'd grown up in Los Angeles with three sisters and he was now married with two kids who were younger than me. And he had a kid who was older, from his previous marriage. I knew he was famous. I saw his records displayed in record stores, and as I grew older, I noticed that I looked more and more like him. I had his "almondine" eyes, as Alan described them. Whenever I saw his name in the *Village Voice* music listings, it was always big. But I also thought that might have been because it was only eight letters. Over the years, my mother had mentioned Roy's self-centeredness, so I was less concerned with what I might say when we spoke, and more curious with what *he* might say. Would he just talk about himself?

That evening, as I watched him in the studio, I could sense that he knew that everyone was focused on him even though his eyes were closed. After he finished recording, Roy and a few more people joined us in the lounge, exchanging hugs and fives. All of these gorgeous, presumably talented men and women seemed so upbeat, so alive. The room radiated with positive energy, and Roy—my father—was the epicenter.

When Roy finally came over to me, the only thing he said was "You want some tempura?" I shook my head and sheepishly said no. Then he walked away, continuing to ask around the room, rounding up the Japanese food order that would soon arrive at the studio.

I suddenly felt very out of place. I hadn't expected an introduction to everyone in the room. But I equally hadn't expected to be placed on the same level as the hired studio engineer who had accepted Roy's tempura offer. There was no part of me that wanted to confront Roy—I'd never been angry with him. But I'd never met an adult who hadn't properly initiated a conversation with me by saying hello. He was my father, and he'd invited me to join him. I couldn't yet process how simple and welcoming the word "hello" could be, but I could process its absence, and my stomach churned with an awkward self-consciousness that, deep down, I knew wasn't my fault.

Alan and I left soon after that.

Roy was busy living his excellent life. He'd had a moment for me. He'd had a few moments for my mother. He was a talented person surrounded by greatness and he appeared to be taking full advantage of all of it. But I wondered why he couldn't sit with me for five minutes during the break and teach me a song. Or ask me something about my life. Or tell me something about his.

On our walk back to Alan's apartment we didn't talk about Roy or the studio. Instead, Alan and I ranked in order the movies we'd seen so far on my New York visit. Was *Airplane!* the best? Yes, we both agreed it was. We talked about music—Alan had recently introduced me to German electronic pioneers Kraftwerk. We ranked the restaurant meals we'd eaten: Macrobiotic rice and vegetables at Souen? Greasy, dense chicken lo mein at Wo Hop? The big ride on his motorcycle to Sheepshead Bay for Italian seafood? Or was it just the sloppy slice from Ben's Pizza on Spring Street?

I wasn't a baseball fan, but when we got home, I reluctantly agreed to watch the Yankees game on TV. Alan, in exchange, agreed to one more trip to Forty-Eighth Street to visit music stores. That was my favorite place in the city. I loved to look at drums and fantasize about owning all of them. We made plans for my next trip to New York, which was probably only a month or two away. Who were the Yankees playing? Should we ride Alan's motorcycle to the Cloisters? Where would we eat?

Even though I didn't realize it then, that evening was my first indication that biology might not totally determine who my father was.

7.

Living for the City

I n the summer of 1981, when I was nine, my mother and I
moved back to New York City, where her UMass MBA had
earned her a job at American Express. They put us up at the
Vista International Hotel for a full month while we looked for
an apartment. The Vista was a brand-new building located directly between the World Trade Center towers in lower Manhattan. We lived in room 741, and I befriended the housekeepers,
who always placed an extra chocolate coin on my pillow and
tucked my stuffed Snoopy into bed as if he were a sleeping guest.
Our room sat seven stories above the giant courtyard in front
of the World Trade Center, which became a playground where I
dodged dark-suited men and women whose taut focus and brisk
pace made me invisible to them.

Once in a while, my mother or Alan took me to the top of the World Trade Center. Every memory I have includes ringing ears from the rocket-ride elevator, which took only thirty seconds to climb 110 stories. Back then, you could pay very little to take the elevator to the top of Tower 1, and from there, you could walk upstairs, outside to the actual roof. The scariest view wasn't across the river to New Jersey or uptown to Central Park—it was the view of the second tower, which stood at the same height, mere yards away, offering a dizzying perspective of how massive, daunting, and powerful the Twin Towers were.

At American Express my mother was earning $28,000 a year—about $82,000 in today's dollars—which we both thought was a ton of money. We found a one-bedroom apartment for $725 on Morton Street just off Hudson Street, a quiet, tree-lined block in the West Village, one of the city's nicest neighborhoods—then and now. We lived across the street from John Belushi's town house and within walking distance from Alan's loft on Canal Street.

I attended fifth grade on scholarship at the Little Red School House, a left-wing private school a short walk from our apartment. Little Red was founded in 1921 as the first ever progressive school in New York City, and in addition to esteemed alumni like Robert De Niro, political activist Angela Davis, and educator and Weather Underground member Kathy Boudin, my mother's cousins Michael and Peter had attended in the forties. My class picture, which still hangs on my wall today, resembles the United Colors of Benetton kids ads that came later that decade: we were a colorful representation of Black, white, Iranian, and Japanese faces, each beaming self-assured smiles.

In New York my friends lived much different lives from the kids I'd known in Amherst. My friend Noah's father actually voted in the Oscars. My friend Andrew's family owned a five-story town house in the West Village, where hide-and-seek was no fun because the house was too big for anyone to ever be found. King Han's parents owned an upscale SoHo restaurant, and his family lived above it in a gigantic loft that had the towering ceilings of a movie set. Annan's family had just emigrated from Israel, and on the first day of fifth grade, she spoke almost no English. Several kids were on scholarship, like me, and some lived in Brooklyn, which at the time felt very far away.

My friends and I had absorbed racial stereotypes from TV, music, and movies, but they were hard to confirm in New York, where they didn't seem to exist in the same way. While we ate Mamoun's falafel and sloppy Italian hero sandwiches from Conca D'oro, I never considered the race of the people serving us. Even when I walked through Washington Square Park, all ethnicities were represented in the drug dealers and their customers, the cops and the pickpockets, the graffiti artists and the street cleaners.

The only difference we did perceive? The appearance of the students at Our Lady of Pompeii, the Catholic school one block away from ours. Not because they were all Italian, but because the boys all looked like the same person to us, each wearing the same perfectly pressed uniforms and matching military-like haircut. Though we tried to avoid them, our shared space was Father Demo Square, a small park between our schools that bordered two pizza places, each of which offered seventy-five-cent slices.

If we were ever in line for pizza next to the uniformed kids, we clammed up. We knew that the Village had been an Italian neighborhood for generations, and our silence felt like an acknowledgment that we were invading their territory. I recall the proprietors offering the uniformed kids special perks, tossing in an Italian accent: "You want some extra *mootzarell*?" With all their clone-like uniforms, I often expected a confrontation—maybe something that would lead to a hard fist in the cheek or stomach, something we all feared. But no altercation ever occurred and no words were ever exchanged. That being said, our silence—even if self-imposed—is my earliest memory of feeling threatened by someone who I perceived as being different, whether it was real or imagined.

ON THE OCCASIONAL WEEKEND, my mother and I would take the subway forty-five minutes out to Flatbush, one of the very Jewish parts of Brooklyn, almost as far as Coney Island. There, we'd spend the day with my great-grandfather Joe and his wife Edith.

The walk from the subway to Grandpa Joe's apartment was a world apart from our Manhattan neighborhood, but it shared certain elements. Kids around my age also played with balls and sticks, but they looked more innocent, as if they'd just left temple in their black pants and untucked white dress shirts. They wore yarmulkes, and their hair, which extended into long, angelic curls, sometimes nearly touched their shoulders. Men and women sat outside on deck chairs, but everyone seemed unfriendly. They looked at my mother and me, but nobody smiled or said hello.

The residents of Flatbush likely had no idea that by Jewish law both my mother and I were Jewish. Instead, we walked the streets feeling judged and unwelcome.

But when we arrived at Grandpa Joe's, we were home. "He's such a schnorrer," Edith would say, describing a neighbor who always asked to borrow things. "She was hocking me a chinik," Joe exclaimed about a former colleague who talked too much. The next winter, when my mother brought me to the doctor with a serious cold, the doctor asked me to describe my symptoms. "I have a *chack* and a *schnoz*," I said in a nasal voice, describing my sore throat and stuffy nose in my own made-up, Yiddish-sounding terms.

Years later, my wife divulged that on one of our early dates, she'd left a family dinner to meet me. When her cousin asked if her date was Jewish like her, she answered no, likely still wondering exactly what I was. Little did she know how meshuga that was. Our wedding included a rabbi, a ketubah, a chuppah, and every other Jewish tradition we could wrangle.

AROUND 1982, ROY PLAYED at the Village Gate. Just like at the UMass concert, my mother and I showed up early before the club was open, hoping to say hi. The dimly lit, empty room smelled of sour alcohol and stale cigarettes, and soon Roy arrived with a woman. He introduced us to her—"This is Louise and Nabil"—but he didn't say who exactly we were, and he didn't introduce the woman. I don't remember what she looked like, but my mother assumed she was Roy's wife.

Like my experience at Electric Lady, I was too young to fully understand how social cues worked, but I knew that Roy's were off, and again I felt somehow left out or skipped over. I don't remember any more of our conversation—it's likely that I tuned out while my mother rambled on about my many successes as a ten-year-old. I never noticed if she was bothered by his detachment or his disinterest, but I could feel resentment starting to bubble up in me.

That day, Roy gave me a round pin with his face on it, and while I loved pins—by now I had them for all of my favorite bands—this one felt different. Was it truly a gift if it was a promotional item that had his face on it?

Later that night, while we waited for Roy's band to play, I started to feel antsy and tired, and I insisted that we leave. When my mother said we should wait and see him play, I said something like, "Well, he wouldn't wait and see me—let's just go." So we left.

That same year, he played again in the Village. My mother and I stood outside as he arrived in a cab, but he was swarmed by people and was quickly whisked off. He didn't even pay attention to us—he just said a quick hi and smiled as he continued walking to the door—so we left. Again. Moments like these became blips on my slowly growing list of disappointing interactions with my father.

My mother never conveyed frustration during these instances or apologized to me on behalf of my distant, uninterested father. And she never apologized for her decision to have me knowing he wouldn't be around—an apology I never expected. My mother's goal remained well intentioned: she simply wanted me to be able to meet him as much as possible, even if only for a minute. I also think that my mother needed to prove to Roy that her desire to raise me on her own had yielded exceptional results: we were more than getting by, we were a happy family. For me, though, interactions like these proved that we were better off without him.

ONE AFTERNOON IN THE VILLAGE, my mother and I ran into a woman whom she introduced as Dr. Manska—a doctor who'd lived on her corner and given her special attention during her pregnancy. Dr. Manska looked at me with a loving smile, reminding me of my grandmother. Then she looked at my mother and spoke kindly with a Russian accent. "I was so worried about you when you were pregnant. You were so young, and alone with no money. But look at you . . . look at you both." Dr. Manska held her arms out and nodded gently with approval. "You did it."

8.

Don't Stop Believin'

In New York City, my mother was being paid well. Even with her student loans, my school tuition, and the high cost of living, we were doing fine. But my mother wasn't happy. She wasn't built for corporate America and she didn't like the pressure or the environment. She had gotten her MBA so she could improve the quality of life for her son and herself, not to rise up in the ranks at American Express. She wasn't competitive in that way. She didn't want it.

After work one evening, my mom brought home an interesting option. American Express was planning to move its entire Travelers Cheques division—where she worked—to Salt Lake City, Utah, home of Donny and Marie Osmond and the Church of Jesus Christ of Latter-day Saints, then commonly referred to as the Mormon church. To a New Yorker, the West was extremely far away. From my limited perspective, even New Jersey seemed like a different world. I'd traveled a lot and met all kinds of people in my ten years, but I'd never left the East Coast.

The thought of making the same amount or more money at American Express in Salt Lake City, a considerably less expensive city, was enticing for my mother though. Utah was very family driven, so work would end at 5:00 p.m., unlike New York, where she often worked into the night. I really wanted to play drums, which was impossible in our New York apartment because of our neighbors and because the drums I'd owned for eight years had deteriorated into rusted and splintered pieces of metal and wood. American Express pitched Salt Lake City as the land of opportunity. We could live an easier life in a big apartment where I could play a brand-new set of drums as much as I wanted.

One night over dinner, my mother, Alan, and I had a conversation about race in Salt Lake City, which we all understood to be an extremely white place. I remember actually saying, "Well, I guess if it's just one state out of fifty, it's okay if they want it to be all white people." Alan snapped back at me—something he rarely did—explaining that no, that would not be okay, and that it was not the case. Alan and I had argued before, but only about what movie to see or where to eat, never over anything like this. I knew that racist people existed, but I'd never realized until this moment that they were factually wrong. Alan's response taught me that there was no room for middle ground—he was right.

. . .

IN MARCH 1982, we flew Western Airlines to visit Salt Lake City to see whether we wanted to relocate. It was the first time I remember being on an airplane, and I was amazed that I could watch a movie while eating a TV dinner. We stayed at a brand-new Marriott hotel downtown, one block from the Mormon temple. The air in Salt Lake felt cleaner, as if I'd unknowingly been breathing through a musty filter for the past year. In New York, the sun beat down like an enemy. Here, the sun felt friendlier and closer—and, at four thousand feet, I suppose it was. It wasn't all perfect. In Salt Lake City, people walked at a leisurely pace that confounded me. Didn't they have someplace to be? But they seemed content, as if they weren't going anywhere—they were already there. And everyone said hello on the street or at least nodded.

Most people in Salt Lake City were blond. But not California blond like in the movies. They had natural golden-blond hair with streaks of brown that looked even cooler because it was so new to me. Nobody seemed to notice my Afro, which was quite large and lumpy at the time. I wondered whether people actually didn't notice that I looked different or if they noticed but just didn't care.

My mom had done some research and had already decided where we'd live if we moved and which school I would attend: Wasatch Elementary. It was in a neighborhood called the Avenues, where all of the streets were letters: A Street, B Street, etc.

I knew that Wasatch was on R Street. The morning of our school visit, our taxi glided up South Temple Street, and I looked out the window watching the signs pass: M Street, N Street, O Street. R Street was coming soon, and I felt the dread in my stomach. Visiting a school was worse than being the new kid. It was *auditioning* to be the new kid.

Wasatch was a modern brick-and-glass building that occupied a full city block. A tunnel led students under a busy street to the playground, which was considerably larger than the school itself and held multiple fields and shiny beams and bars designed for climbing. There was so much grass—something that my school in New York had none of.

Inside the long, spacious hallways, my sneakers squeaked loudly. The gym looked like an NBA court with its shiny, flawless floor and high ceilings.

The principal invited my mother and me to visit a class, and when we entered, I was greeted by stares. I felt like an intruder. I had no idea if I was wearing the right clothes or if my facial expression conveyed the right amount of cool. I noticed the sandy-blond hair on nearly every head. The few dark-haired kids stood out to me, but their cuts and styles were the same as everyone else's: straight, with the occasional curl.

The longer I looked, the more I began to realize why the students had all stared at me for what seemed like an unnecessarily long time. My Afro and darker skin stood out like a kid with an arm cast or crutches. But those exist from injuries—they'd heal and soon return to normal. I would never be normal if it meant having straight, blond hair. I became antsy and the teacher's words sounded like nonsense—just words occupying space. I pulled at my mother's shirt: *Let's go, please. I'm not comfortable here.*

But despite my discomfort, even at ten, I knew that if I had to, I could fit in and make friends anywhere and with anyone. We'd already moved a few times, and Wasatch would be my fourth school since kindergarten. I didn't need other kids with Afros to become my friends; I needed kids of all kinds to not let *my* Afro define me.

Afterward, I didn't need to explain to my mother how I felt— she was more conscious of the blond heads than I was. But she explained that she wanted to try Salt Lake City—that we both needed to be open to it. It would be a better life for both of us in which she would be happier with less stress and more money and I would make great friends instantly. I could visit New York as much as I wanted and Alan would visit us too. And if we really didn't like it, we could always move back to New York.

I believed my mother when she said we could always move back, and I had no doubt that she had both of our best interests at heart. She'd gotten us this far—which was *very* far. New York was family, friends, and culture. It was where I was born and where my mother and my uncle had moved as soon as they were able to. But it wasn't sustainable for us.

That night, my mom took us to a last-minute concert. I didn't know much about the band Journey—all I knew was that they were a rock band and that they were playing down the street from our hotel at the Salt Palace arena. We walked over and joined a crowd of fans who waved their arms and bobbed their heads to every song. Even in clean-living Salt Lake, I noticed the familiar concert smell of pot and cigarette smoke mixed with sweat, alcohol, and youthful endorphins.

Journey had just released their album *Escape*, which opens with the anthem "Don't Stop Believin'." To this day, when I hear that song, I flash back to the moment when my mother and I stood anonymously among twelve thousand people, singing along euphorically to a song that at that moment meant everything to everyone present. To me, it meant not giving up but setting aside everything we knew about New York and Amherst. Family and friends would still exist, we'd just see them less often and talk more on the phone. It meant clean air, grass, and mountains. It meant a less stressful life for my mother and a more musical life for me. During the song's four-minute build, my mother and I felt a connection to the band, to everyone in the room, and we looked at each other, bouncing as we belted out the song's uplifting chorus.

The next day, my mother and I returned home to New York with a plan to move to Salt Lake City that summer.

9.

Super Freak

My mother had never learned to drive, which was imperative in Salt Lake City. So before we relocated, my mother, at thirty-three, took private driving lessons in New York from a gentleman named Bert, who was in his forties with golden skin and slicked-back, grayish-black hair. Bert spoke with the patient New York accent of a veteran city dweller. "Turn, turn, turn, dear," he'd say to my mother as she gripped the wheel and cars zipped past her. I rode along, playing a bleeping handheld video game in the back seat while my mother drove us down the West Side Highway, over the Brooklyn Bridge, and through the lawless streets of New York City in the early eighties.

Sometimes we used my mother's driving lessons as a mode of transportation around New York City. Once after a lesson we got dropped off at her friend Jenny's apartment on the Upper West Side. We joined Jenny to attend a fair at her daughter's school. On the way there, Jenny pointed out that it was the same private school Roy's other kids attended, but it didn't occur to me that we might run into them.

While I was aware Roy had other children, I never thought about them. They were even more distant than Roy—people I knew existed but whom I'd never met or even seen in a photograph. To me, they weren't my siblings, they were just Roy's other kids.

That day was a perfect, sunny and warm—but not hot or humid—New York spring afternoon. The fair resonated with laughter, brightly colored clothing, and balloons. Children, parents, and faculty crowded the school's parklike grounds, which were populated with grass patches, paved paths, and booths that filled the air with the smell of sweet, greasy fried things.

Walking lazily downhill on a small path, we ran right into Roy and, I quickly presumed, his family. A boy and a girl—younger, shorter, and darker skinned than I—stood before me with blank stares.

Roy looked different, but I still immediately recognized the familiar swagger and confidence I'd seen before. Whoever surrounded him—his band, his friends, his family—they were with *him*. As usual, my mother was inquisitive, engaging, and complimentary. "Ooh, I like your hair, what's different?"

Roy smiled and felt his hair between his fingers. "I'm playing with Rick James so I've gotta have braids." At the time, Rick James was best known for his 1981 funk-disco smash "Super

Freak." Rick had just released the single "Dance wit' Me" in April 1982, on which Roy played a solo.

Roy didn't introduce us to the woman or children that were with him. The whole encounter felt more like an interaction between my mother and someone she knew from a previous job—an exchange of pleasantries and a quick hello.

The kids and I studied each other shyly. That day, I distinctly remember thinking those kids were lucky to be with him. In my limited experience, being with Roy was like walking into a room with the most popular person—everyone sees you with them and immediately thinks more of you.

Looking back now, I wonder how my father felt—what it was like for him to run into us with his family. Was there a part of him that panicked and thought, *These children are all related—through me—should I tell them?* He didn't seem panicked. On the contrary, he seemed as cool as ever. My guess is that he was happy to be recognized and to accept compliments from my mother.

If I could revisit that moment now, I like to think that I'd point out the elephant in the room and say, "Who cares about your braids? How about acknowledging the fact that the two people standing in front of me are my brother and sister, whom I've never met?" But with the agreement my mother made with him all those years ago, would I even have the right to ask him that question?

10.

Searching

Salt Lake City felt magical in the summer—an arid, desert heat with burning pink-and-orange sunsets—versus the steaming, muggy New York summers that I had wanted to pass more quickly. Still, I had a hard time adjusting to the quiet of a smaller city, especially at night, when there was so little outside noise that I sometimes had difficulty falling asleep.

There were other changes, though, that were easier to accept. Until then we'd only had a small black-and-white television. Suddenly we had a color TV and a real stereo. We also had cable TV, which included HBO, a channel that showed movies all the time, with no commercials in the middle. We'd always owned rickety hand-me-down furniture, but now, for the first time in my life, we owned a new couch and dining room table. All of this was courtesy of American Express's generous "home find-ing" package, a bonus they gave each of the many New Yorkers who moved to Salt Lake City.

My mother had passed her driving test before we left New York, and we had a brand-new 1982 blue Subaru hatchback. In-stead of shopping for dinner every night in a few specialty shops, we went to one giant store on the weekend and bought every-thing we needed—so much that we sometimes had to make two trips to get the bags from the car to our apartment. I noticed that we suddenly paid with real cash or sometimes a check, not the Monopoly-money-like food stamps I'd grown accustomed to in Amherst. I ran up long-distance phone bills calling Alan in New York every day, and occasionally my grandparents in Long Is-land. And I had piles of Legos. Life was good.

During this time, we attended a few suburban social func-tions in the homes of American Express employees who wanted to welcome all the newcomers with kids to Salt Lake City. These events reminded me of Baha'i functions in Cambridge and Am-herst: nobody drank and there was tons of food. I was offered hot dogs and ambrosia—which I learned was a Jell-O salad with millet, canned fruit, and whipped cream—foods that, even though they were as American as you can get, felt curious and foreign to me.

In these homes, framed photographs of huge families hung on mantels above fireplaces. They looked like the TV show *The Waltons*: all blond, all clean-cut, each a younger or older version of the person next to them. The photos reminded me of the ones that come in cheap frames at the drugstore.

They also served as a reminder that my mother and I were alone together. Not a single photograph of me, my mother, and my father together existed.

WE BEGAN TO ACCLIMATE to Salt Lake City's culture. My mom taught me to be open-minded, and we went to everything, including the Days of '47 Rodeo, which celebrated the arrival of the first Mormon pioneers to the Salt Lake Valley in 1847; Mormon church picnics when our neighbors invited us; and business dinners with my mom's American Express coworkers. We were skeptical of Salt Lake City at first, but everyone we met was kind and accepting, which pleasantly contradicted the warnings we'd heard before moving.

This included our neighbor Ron. In Salt Lake I had a brand-new drum set in my room that I played every day, which our neighbors, shockingly, tolerated. One day, Ron knocked on our door. It turned out he was the principal timpanist in the Utah Symphony and was hoping to meet the other drummer in the building. He soon became one of our closest family friends. He once brought me to Salt Lake's elegant Symphony Hall during the afternoon and I played his timpani on the giant stage, where the loud notes rang out forever among 2,800 empty seats. Even without an audience, I felt the electrifying buzz of performance.

My school was about 60 percent Mormon. Everyone got along well and religion wasn't a dividing line between students. The Mormon church had only just welcomed Black men into its priest-hood four years prior in 1978. But to my surprise, I wasn't the only non-white kid at Wasatch Elementary School. There were Chinese, Japanese, and Mexican kids, and some from Tonga and Samoa, two Polynesian islands, where the Mormons sent missionaries.

I did my best to blend in with my classmates, and fortunately, I'd had the summer to absorb fashion trends, radio stations, and the new pronunciation of words I thought I knew. "Orange" was a completely different word in Salt Lake, which began with "or" instead of "ar," as it had in New York. "Pop" referred to the sugary, carbonated canned beverage that I'd known for my entire life as "soda." I spent the summer listening to KRSP, a scratchy AM radio station that ingrained current hits into my head, like the Human League's "Don't You Want Me," Survivor's "Eye of the Tiger," and the drum-solo-infected "Jack & Diane" by John Cougar. And I bought all the right clothes, including two Ocean Pacific (OP) brand shirts. OP made California surf wear that looked foreign, exotic, and far beyond my comprehension. I felt like a fraud the first time I wore my tan OP polo, which had bright horizontal orange and turquoise stripes. But my hesitation disappeared when every kid—as if they were *required* to—said, "Nice OP shirt!" I also learned never to wear Sears Toughskins jeans. Toughskins were the dead giveaway of a low-income family, and that was the last way I wanted anyone to think of me.

But despite all my efforts to fit in, nobody else looked like me. All of my friends were white. And for the first time in my life, people asked me if I was adopted. It was a question I'd never gotten before, but one my mother heard often when I was a baby in the very Italian Greenwich Village. The question felt intrusive, and each time I'd answer, feeling confrontational, "No, I just look more like my father." I knew that wasn't exactly true: my mother and I have often been told how similarly we smile. Even then, my defensive response made me feel bad—like I was abandoning my obvious maternal traits in order to appease someone who only saw my Afro and the color of my skin. But I kept answering that way.

A white classmate once got up the nerve to ask me, "Nabil, are you poor?" I didn't know how to respond. I knew that we had less money than many of the two-parent, home-owning families in my class. But I wore the same preppy Polo shirts, plaid Bermuda shorts, and Sperry Topsiders as everyone else. Then I realized she'd asked me the question because of my race—or the race she had decided I belonged to.

These questions never seemed to change anyone's opinion of me. It's possible that the lack of Blackness in Salt Lake City somehow qualified me as "safe": with no obvious stereotypes in place, I became a nonthreatening, exotic ally. I eventually learned to let the small transgressions, like requests to touch my Afro, roll over me—justifying them as not ill intentioned. If anyone asked, I said that my parents were divorced—something that still held a stigma in Salt Lake, but less so, and with less explanation than the truth. I never called anybody out when they asked if I was adopted or if I was poor. But internally, I wasn't completely at ease. I absorbed the burden of explaining that I wasn't adopted or poor, which became a tiresome reminder that no matter how much I thought I fit in, I was still different.

. . .

THOUGH SALT LAKE SEEMED LIKE a normal, all-American city, it had a very dark recent history. When we moved there in 1982, four boys had been sexually assaulted and murdered, and their killer was on the loose. So during my first week of sixth grade, every student was forced to give fingerprints and hair samples so that if something happened, our potential corpses could be more quickly and easily identified.

This terrified me, having just moved from New York City, ostensibly one of the most dangerous places in America. In New York, I walked home from school alone, crossing the insanely busy Sixth Avenue. My friends and I spent time in Washington Square Park surrounded by drug dealers and their customers. We knew what bad people looked like and how to avoid them, and nobody ever bothered us.

Now, three months later, in the most family-friendly place on earth, where nobody looked like a bad person, I was told I couldn't go *anywhere* alone, *ever*. Everyone had to have at least one partner to walk home with or had to be picked up by a parent after school. We weren't allowed to talk to anyone we didn't know or to give strangers directions. If a car slowed down or seemed to be getting close, we were instructed to *run, immediately*, in the opposite direction.

My friends and I had a genuine fear of being kidnapped. It wasn't something that happened far away that was occasionally reported on the news—it was really happening around us, with regularity, to people my friends had known. The Atlanta murders of 1979–81, in which more than two dozen young people had gone missing and been found murdered, were also recent. And like the Atlanta murders—in which every victim was Black—the Salt Lake City victims all had something in common: they were all white boys. But whereas the Atlanta victims were described as "Black boys," the Salt Lake City victims were described simply as "boys" because their whiteness was assumed.

I knew about the Atlanta case and I was aware of this difference, which made me feel safer. I actually envisioned my friends Matt and Nathan—both white—and me walking home from school when a dark van slowly pulled up. As if in a movie, a windowless door would quickly slide open, and two figures wearing black ski masks would appear, snatching my friends and disappearing as quickly as they arrived. The van would peel off and I'd be left standing on a quiet Salt Lake City street with two backpacks sloppily spilled on the ground on either side of me—the only remaining evidence of my two friends. And before I could think to shout for help, I'd think, *Thank god they didn't want me.*

11.

Ebony and Ivory

When we moved to Salt Lake City in 1982, MTV was just one year old: a twenty-four-hour cable TV channel that reached millions of people and played nothing but music videos. If I wanted to hear a song more than once, I'd place my Radio Shack cassette recorder next to the tiny speaker of our TV. Toward the end of a video, I'd rest my fingers anxiously above both the record and play buttons, ready to push them if they played Van Halen's chugging anthem "Unchained" or X's thundering, bluesy "The Hungry Wolf." The music I heard and saw on MTV—at a time when my frame of reference was so fresh and limited, a time when I was so musically malleable—shaped my taste for the rest of my life.

Sometimes MTV was actually live on the air. I'll never forget an interview with the Guyanese British singer Eddy Grant when his dance-reggae hit "Electric Avenue" was being played constantly.

"Eddy, what do you think of MTV?" asked the host, smiling arrogantly against a distracting early eighties backdrop.

"I think you should turn that *M* over and make it a *W* for White TV," said Grant, without hesitation.

More than anything, I wanted to be the drummer in a band on MTV. But up until then, I hadn't stopped to notice that MTV played predominantly white artists, with a few exceptions: Eddy Grant and Musical Youth, a band of young Jamaican kids who filled an odd reggae slot. Paul McCartney and Stevie Wonder's "Ebony and Ivory" was an early attempt at unity. But Michael Jackson had not yet dominated MTV with *Thriller.* When it started, MTV was a rock music channel. And rock music was white. I didn't want to be in Earth Wind & Fire or the Commodores, two great bands in which Afros seemed imperative. I wanted to be in a rock band—playing with Rush or Pat Benatar.

But the stars I admired didn't have Afros. I began to worry mine would hold me back.

WHEN I WAS IN sixth grade, Def Leppard released their third album, *Pyromania.* Several of the band's videos were on MTV, and the songs blew my mind with their shrill guitars and their pounding, futuristic drums. When the British band announced a Salt Lake City show in the summer of 1983, my mother and I waited in line for hours to get a pair of tickets.

On the afternoon of the show, my mother took me to stand outside by the back loading gate of the Salt Palace arena. An eleven-year-old boy and his mother were of no interest to the security guard, whose job it was to lazily shuffle away the more obvious fans who shared our idea. After about twenty minutes, a van pulled up, and the five members of Def Leppard emerged with a few handlers. I immediately noticed how young the band members looked, each of them skinny, pale, and grinning ear to ear as they squinted in the desert sun.

I pointed out Rick Allen, the nineteen-year-old drummer, and my mom walked right up to him and said quite simply, "Hi, Rick. My son is a drummer and he'd really like to meet you." The entourage walked through a heavy iron gate, and as the security guard put his arm out to stop my mom and me, Rick said softly in a British accent, "These guys are all right."

While the rest of the band went inside, we stood outside with Rick for a few valuable minutes. He and I talked about our favorite drummers: I liked Neil Peart, Terry Bozzio, and him. He liked Keith Moon and John Bonham. Rick showed me his left hand, which had a bump so large next to his pinkie it almost looked like he was growing a sixth finger. This, he explained, was from playing traditional grip, which was rare for a rock drummer. *This guy*, I thought—from MTV, from the radio, from the biggest band in the world—*is so kind and down-to-earth*.

Def Leppard played everything I wanted to hear that night. But I felt anxious the entire show. Not with nausea but with a deep sense of scary anticipation. I went to the bathroom a few times, just so I could stare at myself in the mirror, wondering if maybe, someday, I could do what Rick did.

DAVE, AN UPBEAT TWENTYSOMETHING with a scruffy beard, was my first drum teacher. I'd already been playing for nearly a decade but was completely self-taught, and my mother and I thought it would be good to have some instruction from a real live drummer. Dave was the best drummer in the city and we'd seen him play several times. I remember thinking that this skinny, normal guy was so impressive once onstage behind a drum set. He obviously belonged there and nowhere else. I wanted people to think that way about me, and I hoped Dave could help.

Dave was white, but he introduced me to the music of lots of non-white drummers, not because of my race, but because Omar Hakim, Jack DeJohnette, and several other Black and Latin drummers were responsible for the most exciting drumming at the time. Although I was less connected than ever to Black culture on a personal level, that didn't have to be the case in my musical life.

Rather than adjusting my self-taught background to one of disciplined practice, Dave quickly adapted to what he thought I needed. We had weekly sessions in which he introduced me to new music and either watched me teach myself how to play it or helped me figure it out. I recall several friendly arguments with Dave about how a particular part was played, and his frustration in realizing that I, an eleven-year-old, was right. And I remember the revelatory feeling of learning that someone else could teach me more than I could teach myself.

Dave also taught me how to play guitar, which felt unnatural and impossible. It was like I was seven years old and holding Eduardo's electric guitar all over again. But Dave assured me, "Once you get it, you'll never remember not getting it," and his easygoing manner convinced me I could do it. He was right, and in addition to the Devo and Van Halen riffs I figured out on my own, Dave taught me colorful jazz chords and twangy blue-grass songs that required intricate picking. Once I knew a few basic chords, guitar—like drums—came naturally to me. I never stopped to think why I quickly eclipsed my friends who had taken guitar lessons for years. But in retrospect, I can't help but think about my father—the influence of someone who was never around but who was always present in my DNA.

THERE WERE SEVERAL world-class ski resorts within forty-five minutes of Salt Lake, so everyone with means was a skier. I'd taken a few lessons during my first winter there. I'd always loved the snow, and the thrill of speeding down a hill with the lack of fear only a ten-year-old can possess was addictive. But it wasn't as addictive as music.

Once I realized that there was only enough money to either ski or buy records and musical gear, the choice was easy. I had a drum set but I didn't have the Zildjian eight-inch splash cymbal that Stewart Copeland played all over Police albums. I didn't have the space-age Remo Rototoms that Terry Bozzio played in Missing Persons. The thought of owning any of these was even more enticing than racing down a snow-covered mountain.

My mother offered another solution: I could become a child actor, specifically in TV commercials. I loved the idea. I couldn't act, but would I really need to for a thirty-second commercial? I wasn't shy. And surely there was a lot of money to be made. Plus I had a "unique look," according to my mother and the casting agent she'd recently met through a colleague. I'd stand out among all of the blond kids.

My first audition was forty-five minutes south of Salt Lake in Orem, Utah, at Osmond Studios, where the seventies variety show *Donny & Marie* had been shot.

A horde of blond stage moms and their blonder kids lined up at the registration table. It reminded me of the day I visited my potential school in Salt Lake—like everyone else had experience and I was the one who stood out. I glanced around the lobby, sizing up the competition: blue-eyed drops of perfection who *looked* like they should be in TV commercials.

After check-in I was ushered into a smaller room with a newly carpeted floor and walls of windows. Six of us—five blonds and me—were each given a line and told we were going to play a board game based on the band Duran Duran. I knew the band well from MTV, especially their hit song "Rio."

When it was my turn, I picked up a pair of cold plastic dice and shook them carefully. Then I opened up my hands, allowing the dice to spill sloppily on the board as the busy bassline from "Rio" played in my head.

"Oh no! Rio!" I tossed my hands in the air and shouted my line with my most convincing excited-meets-disappointed smile.

I didn't get the gig. Nor did I get the next one, which would have had me skiing down a mountain with an animated Tony the Tiger on our way to a big, satisfying bowl of Frosted Flakes. I'd felt even more out of place at the Frosted Flakes audition, which took place at the Snowbird ski resort and put me up against blond, blue-eyed kids who could ski well, something I couldn't do.

A few months later, when I saw the Frosted Flakes commercial on TV, I didn't think, *That should have been me.* When I saw racially mixed people on TV, the scene was usually about their race—they could never just exist. Even Tony the Tiger—who was mostly orange with black stripes—sounded like a white man. So I didn't expect to see him skiing with anyone other than a white kid.

12.

Manny's Music

Back then, one of my favorite places in the world—and New York was still the world to me—was Forty-Eighth Street between Sixth and Seventh Avenues: home of several famous musical instrument stores, including Sam Ash and Manny's. When I lived in Salt Lake City, I used to call Sam Ash's toll-free number after school, sometimes multiple times in a week. The same guy always answered.

"Sam Ash," he'd say, his low New York–accented voice raised on the word Ash as if he were introducing Sam Ash himself. I'd rattle through a list of products I'd seen in *Musician* magazine, asking for prices even though I had no realistic need to know them. Once he called me "ma'am," making me hyper-aware that my eleven-year-old voice was still quite high. But even though the exercise was fantasy, it helped me feel connected to New York, my home away from home.

ONE HOT SUMMER DAY in 1983 when I was visiting New York, Alan and I were on our way out of Manny's Music, leaving a cacophony of guitar skronks, keyboard licks, drum crashes, and PA announcements in our wake as we walked down the front stairs of the multilevel superstore.

"Hey, how you doing?" Alan said to someone.

We often ran into musicians Alan knew when we visited these stores, and his sincere greeting once again meant we were meeting someone he liked.

A smiling man bounced up the stairs toward us, and he met Alan with a handshake.

"You remember Roy." Alan looked down at me, half asking and half telling me who this man was.

"Hi." I had no idea who he was. Just one year earlier I'd known exactly who he was when we ran into him at that school fair, but now, after a year living in Salt Lake City where he didn't exist, my life had changed so drastically that I'd completely removed him from my consciousness. His name—Roy—didn't register.

"I hear you're in Salt Lake City?" The man looked at me from one stair below, making my height not terribly unequal to his.

"Yeah." *Who is this person and how does he know that I live in Salt Lake City?* I wondered. My answers were short. I wasn't used to Alan's friends talking to me, only to him.

"How are things out there?" He seemed genuinely interested in knowing.

"Good, I guess." My hands were in my pockets now.

Alan and the man talked for another minute before we each said good-bye. When the door closed behind us, I asked Alan, "Who was that and how does he know so much about me?"

"That was *Roy.*" It was then I understood we'd just been talking to my father.

Alan didn't reply with any regret. His tone didn't suggest that we should go back, *now* that I knew I'd just run into my father. He didn't stop on the sidewalk and turn around to reintroduce us. Much like my mother, Alan was okay with the short interactions, and we just kept walking.

Looking back now, I realize that that was the only childhood interaction with my father in which I had his attention. He didn't appear to be too busy or in a hurry, and he asked real questions about my life. He seemed happy, relaxed, and unusually available. But his questions made me uncomfortable because I had no idea who he was.

My own discomfort had likely prodded Alan to wrap up our conversation. But I wish that one of the adults had suggested we go to lunch right there and then. Not make plans for a future date—I know that likely wouldn't have worked out. But in that moment, when my father appeared to be relaxed and available, I wish someone had had the foresight to suggest that our conversation continue.

Maybe it was because he finally showed some interest, but after that moment, I realized I wanted to know more about my father, how it felt to walk into those music stores and buy whatever he wanted, what it was like to travel the world and play music for a living. And I wanted my father to know more about me. I wanted to tell him which albums were my favorites to play along with on the drums, and how exciting it was to win a recent five-kilometer race—and that it was even more exciting to hear my name announced, followed by loud applause as I claimed my ribbon.

The few times I'd been in my father's presence, I was drawn to him. Now I felt it more than ever, and for the first time, I recognized our shared energy and our common interest as we stood on those music store stairs. I wanted to be one of the people my father showed interest in. I wanted to walk into rooms with him and allow his presence to frame me—to help dictate who I was. I wanted to live in the sunshine.

13.

Meat Is Murder

In 1983, Alan finally left 501 Canal Street for a real, adult apartment: a modern loft on West Twenty-Sixth Street in Chelsea, a more central and vibrant neighborhood. The second-floor apartment had every amenity that Canal Street didn't: heat, air-conditioning, and a well-lit stairway that wasn't at risk of collapsing. The reason? Shannon, a woman my mother had introduced him to in Salt Lake City and who had moved to New York to be with him.

Soon enough, Alan and Shannon got married and I had a new aunt.

I was in awe of Shannon. She'd been raised largely in the Southern California alternative community Synanon, which started as a drug rehabilitation center in the 1950s, then evolved into a scandalous, cultish, tax-exempt organization. Shannon had sky-dived several times and claimed to have broken more than twelve bones in her body. But she wasn't fragile. Shannon was and still is a tough, five-foot-four woman with a deep love of adventure, honesty, and confrontation. She introduced me to a feistiness and a directness that I'd never experienced before, contradicting my mother's and Alan's peaceful dispositions and serving as a different, complementary role model.

Suddenly, I had *three* parents. If I found myself needing advice, I had more than enough guidance to choose from.

My mother: "Oh, wow, that's a tough decision. You should really take some time and think about it. I don't want to tell you what to do. You need to really do what you think is right. Do you want something to eat?"

Alan: "I'm sure you'll figure it out, Nabs. You always do the right thing."

Shannon: "Nabs, you need to just bite the fucking bullet and do it."

I usually followed Shannon's advice and still do.

WHEN I VISITED NEW YORK, Shannon and I would walk around the Village and drink iced coffee—which tasted like an adult beverage—outside at Caffè Dante on muggy summer nights. We talked about drinking alcohol (something Shannon did, but my mother and uncle have never done), drugs, and girls—topics I wasn't comfortable discussing with my mother for fear that she'd worry about me.

When I found out that one of my favorite bands, Missing Persons, was playing at the Beacon Theatre in New York while I was visiting, I had to go. Missing Persons had never played in Salt Lake, despite being from nearby LA. Three of the band's members—including my drummer idol, Terry Bozzio—had been in Frank Zappa's band. These were consummate musicians writing and playing extremely strange and technical music who just happened to work for MTV, largely due to singer Dale Bozzio's propensity to perform in a clear plastic top.

Shannon and I rushed uptown to buy tickets at the box office, where, surprisingly, there was no line.

"Hi, can we please get your two best tickets for Missing Persons." I expected the clerk to tell us it was sold out.

"I have two in the second row." The clerk delivered the incredible news with no inflection, obviously numb to how happy he could make people in his job. Shannon slid a Visa card through the small opening in the glass window. "We only take cash. You can charge by phone." Shannon shook her head and mumbled to herself, clearly frustrated, as she searched her wallet for bills.

Shannon nodded toward the clerk's phone. "I don't have enough cash. If I charge by phone, do you just pick up that phone and take my credit card?"

"No, you get the ticket office."

I could sense Shannon's irritation growing.

"Well then, can I please use your phone to call the ticket office so I can buy the tickets I just came all the way uptown to buy?" She sounded like she was reprimanding a bad employee.

"I can't let—"

"Give me the fucking phone!" Shannon cut him off before he could finish. The clerk's hands jumped, as if connected to Shannon's voice by a wire. He dialed the number and passed the receiver to Shannon under the glass. I was impressed, and I felt suddenly removed, as if watching an intense scene in a movie. With the phone in her hand, Shannon turned to me and cracked a subtle smile that said, *Sometimes you have to fight for the people you love.*

THE NEXT YEAR, in the summer of 1985, I was back at the Beacon Theatre, this time with Alan to see the Smiths. Alan and I saw a lot of bands that only I liked, but the Smiths were one that Alan had also been exposed to and loved. I never felt guilty at the concerts that were just for me, but I was especially excited to see a band with my uncle that he also loved. The Smiths had just released their album *Meat Is Murder* and had quickly sold out two nights at the Beacon. We felt lucky to have scored tickets for the second night from Bleecker Bob's, a famous record store in the Village.

But that night, when Alan and I arrived at the theater, the clerk explained that our tickets were for *last night*. Alan insisted that these were the tickets Bleecker Bob's had sold him for tonight, but the clerk wouldn't let us in. From his point of view, we appeared to be scamming our way in with tickets from a concert that had already happened.

I was crushed: I would never see the Smiths, a band that I suspected would never play Salt Lake.

Alan insisted that we go back to Bleecker Bob's—which was far downtown—to explain our situation. The opener, Billy Bragg, hadn't yet started, but when we hopped back on the subway, I felt sure we wouldn't be returning uptown to the Beacon.

The notorious, curmudgeonly record store owner Bleecker Bob occupied the counter, looking bored in the empty store that was about to close for the night. Alan explained that he'd sold us tickets for the wrong night, but Bleecker Bob didn't seem to care, telling Alan there was nothing he could do—he didn't have any tickets for tonight's sold-out show. But Alan wouldn't give up. The conversation escalated and Bleecker Bob raised his voice at Alan, who responded calmly, "I'm not yelling at you, you don't need to yell at me."

With that statement, Alan shifted the entire tone of the conversation, which caused Bleecker Bob to recoil with a surprised look on his face. I'd never seen anyone handle conflict in this way. Alan, a black belt in aikido who was 100 percent in the right in my mind, had de-escalated the situation with one reasonable sentence. Though I didn't know aikido, I knew a lot about it from the classes I witnessed with Alan and more recently from Shannon, who had begun training too.

Aikido, Alan explained, was more defensive than offensive, a graceful martial art in which an opponent's negative energy was sometimes used against them more than one's own. Alan's interaction with Bleecker Bob felt like the principles of aikido at work in a nonphysical confrontation. It showed me the persuasion embedded in rationality, the power that's wrapped up in letting down one's guard and lowering the stakes rather than raising them. Bleecker Bob had been disarmed, peacefully.

"Look, I'll write you a note. That's the best I can do." Bleecker Bob looked as if he wanted to apologize but couldn't quite muster up the nerve. He wrote a quick, sloppy note in blue ink on store letterhead:

These guys got tickets for the wrong night. I feel bad for the kid.

With my expectations still very low, we took the train back uptown. Alan, being a musician, knew to try the stage door rather than returning to the ticket clerk. He handed our bad tickets and Bleecker Bob's note to a thick bouncer who read it but never said a word. He simply looked at Alan, looked at me, and made a gesture with his head to walk through the stage door.

We emerged from a narrow, dimly lit hallway into a bright, fluorescent-lit wing of the backstage area. And there stood all four members of the Smiths, about to walk onstage. I was stunned beyond words, focusing on the twenty-one-year-old guitarist Johnny Marr—a boyish wire of a man with an unmistakably British shag of straight black hair covering most of his pale face.

The Smiths opened their set with the reverb-drenched dirge "Meat Is Murder." The band was barely visible under deliberately dim lighting, and their energy compounded over a ninety-minute set that included almost no breaks between songs and culminated with dozens of audience members dancing onstage with the band. I left bearing the weight of the music, and with the feeling that even though I hadn't actually met the Smiths, I was one step closer to doing what they did.

On the subway home, I thought about what I would have done that night if I'd been in Alan's position—if it had been me with my nephew. I most likely would have given up when Bleecker Bob said he couldn't help me—I certainly wouldn't have escalated the argument. (A decade later, Bleecker Bob was immortalized in an episode of *Seinfeld*, in which an argument became so heated that he jumped over the counter and grabbed a customer by the neck, demonstrating what could have happened if Alan hadn't calmed things down.) What Alan had done that night wasn't in my toolbox at the time. But now, after seeing his calm, rational conversation land us backstage within touching distance of the Smiths, I'd learned a new approach.

14.

Gigantic

When I started at East High School in Salt Lake City in the fall of 1985, I was one of the youngest kids in my class—a lanky, wide-eyed thirteen-year-old boy wandering crowded hallways with men and women. Ronald Reagan was in the middle of his two-term presidency, New Coke had just been introduced, and Black Flag and the Dead Kennedys were pushing hard against Madonna and "We Are the World."

I found East High School intimidating: four stories of stone built in 1913 that looked like an impenetrable government fortress. Dozens of windows dotted its full-block width. From inside my homeroom, the Wasatch Mountains towered above Salt Lake City, where miles of snowcapped peaks distracted students from our classes. Other freshmen casually mentioned locations like the science building and the storied, no-longer-accessible swimming pool as if they'd always known them, thanks to their older siblings. To me, the building's decades of add-ons resembled a complex labyrinth.

But by sophomore year, I had finally adjusted. It helped that four hundred new freshmen now existed below me. I also had a solid group of friends—some of whom were getting their driver's licenses. I knew my way around the complicated school building and now had a locker on the second floor, not in the basement. I was headed into my second season running cross-country, and my times improved in every weekly competition. When the season ended, I discovered beer, pot, and girls. Most important, I played drums in a rock band.

I'd been trying to start a real band since I was five—and I'd come close with my friends in Amherst—but in high school there were finally other kids who were interested and could actually play their instruments. My classmates Dan and Eddie—who played guitar and bass, respectively—and I played songs by punk bands like Minor Threat and the Vandals—both of which I found to be simple and boring from a drumming standpoint. I was more into intricate and technical drummers like Neal Peart of Rush and Billy Cobham of the Mahavishnu Orchestra.

However, when Dan, Eddie, and I finally locked in as a band, my feelings of musical boredom were quickly replaced by feelings of power and freedom that I'd never experienced before. For the first time I had the ability to actually control the sound. I wasn't playing along with a record. If we wanted to play faster, we played faster. If we wanted to play the chorus four times instead of two, we played it four times instead of two. When Dan's entry-level Peavey guitar amp seemed too quiet to him, he turned it up, blasting a wall of distorted sound at me. And the more he cranked up the amp, the more his strumming arm flailed and his blond bangs shook. Eddie's bass amp wasn't huge, but it was big enough to send rumbling sound waves into my body via my drum seat.

To begin a song, I clicked my sticks four times and shouted, "One, two, three, four!" We'd all seen enough bands and videos to know that's how you started a song. Sometimes we sounded like a mess, but during the moments of synchronicity, we felt unstoppable, like we were removing training wheels from a bike and riding really, really fast for the first time. Making it through a full song was fun, but it was even more fun when someone messed up and we had to start again, because I got to count us in again and feel the impact of that first hit, which—no matter where the song went—I could count on as an explosive, emotionally satisfying beginning.

And then we got a lead singer. Alex was the precocious son of a liberal single mother; naturally, he and I hit it off immediately. Alex was already talking about college, and he typically ended conversations with a lively, animated "Tschüss," German for goodbye. Alex was as comfortable with a microphone as he was in his everyday life, which is saying a lot, and it immediately made us a real band. He suggested our name Motion Sickness not by speaking it, but by drawing a morbid logo dripping with something that resembled blood more than it resembled the name's presumed inspiration: vomit.

Motion Sickness went on to play the circuit: high school parties and assemblies. We became known for our covers of the cow-punk "Urban Struggle" by the Vandals, Minor Threat's rendition of "Good Guys (Don't Wear White)," and the surf-rock staple "Walk, Don't Run."

Our first show was at a high school party where we arrived through the back door only moments after the host's parents exited through the front. My hands felt clammy on my sticks just before our first song. But I became less nervous when I noticed the excitement in the room—people wanted to like us before we even started. I felt even better when my bandmates and I made eye contact. We were a unit—a gang—which offered safety and protection. Our show turned out to be even more fun than practice. We played loud and fast, fueled by our own excitement and the drunk grins of the teenagers moshing in front of us. I also loved what happened between our sets, when I was immediately surrounded by a few kids I recognized from school but had never spoken to. One of them handed me a beer and they showered me with compliments. They asked questions about when we'd play our next show and if we were planning to record an album.

When it was time to play again, I held up my beer—something I'd likely learned from TV—and everyone sloppily pushed their cups into mine, covering our hands in foam. For the first time, I understood why many people play team sports and in bands. People depended on me. I had a purpose: to do something I loved and to do it for others.

As our catalog of other bands' songs grew, so did our own. One afternoon, we set up a cassette player and recorded songs that our friends and parents insisted should have been on the radio, like the urgent "Lake Bonneville," which Alex wrote about a prehistoric lake that once covered Utah, and the hokey "BBQ Madness," which was about . . . madness at a BBQ. The next day at school, after a late-night tape-dubbing session and a trip to Kinko's to copy the hand-drawn covers, we persuaded our friends to buy our tape. By the end of the day, we'd sold out of the five-dollar Motion Sickness tape. Like the one-dollar concert I'd put on as a little kid in Amherst, the recording, duplicating, and selling of our tape was another natural step into the music business. I found it just as exhilarating as playing music.

TOWARD THE END of my sophomore year, I got a job as a dish-washer at a little French restaurant called Liaison. At fifteen, I'd already worked two prior jobs: as a delivery boy for my mother's friend's sandwich shop, where I ran lunches to law firms and pro-fessional businesses downtown, and as a stock boy at our neigh-borhood health food store, mopping the floor, cleaning up spills, and dumping heavy sacks of grain into more manageable self-serve bins for $3.35 an hour, the minimum wage at the time.

At Liaison, I spent my afternoons in the kitchen, wearing a messy, once-white apron, operating a small industrial dishwasher. The owner, Bub, was a pleasure to work with and, much like an artist or a musician, he was both a creative genius and an orga-nizational mess. But he haphazardly whipped up perfect dishes: lightly battered trout fillets; creamy, steaming risottos; and but-tered but never mushy vegetables.

Jared, the nineteen-year-old sous-chef, worked the same day shifts as I did. He skateboarded to work and spent most of his time chopping vegetables, marinating meats, and preparing for the restaurant's much busier dinner business. I had a hard time deciding whether Jared was metal or punk, an important distinction in the summer of 1987. He had long hair but he didn't care for it like a metal guy would: it was sloppy and cool, not fluffed or even combed. He loved Metallica, but he also wore Misfits and Black Flag T-shirts.

Jared introduced me to two of my favorite albums: Guns N' Roses' *Appetite for Destruction* and Descendents' *All*. Both albums were played at very high volume in the kitchen, which somehow never bothered Bub or the restaurant's patrons. I appreciated our janky cassette player, which was powerful enough to be heard over the dishwasher in my separate quarters—a small, garbage-smelling lair three steps below the kitchen. I heard those albums so many times that summer, in that setting, that hearing them now—without that crispy distortion, and without the smell of a recently discarded French lunch—doesn't feel quite right.

When Jared left without notice, I was quickly promoted to assistant chef and dishwasher. I learned how to hold a chef's knife while dicing celery. I learned that when whisking together a sauce or a batter, the order of the ingredients is almost as important as the ingredients themselves. And I learned that it's not easy to run a business. Bub spent each day juggling between cooking, dealing with staff, placating vendors, and glad-handing customers.

My afternoons at Liaison were some of the best of my life. When Bub waved a five-dollar bill at me, I knew it meant to run out to the gas station because someone had ordered a Coke. When Bub and a server got into a loud altercation, I knew I'd probably never see her again. When Jared handed me a cold beer toward the end of my shift, it didn't mean *Let's party*. It meant *Thank you for liking the music I play all day and putting up with this crazy place*. It also meant that the guy with the long hair wearing the Slayer T-shirt liked me. I respected Jared and his musical taste, and on top of the fact that I was now in a band, Jared's approval was an early signal that I was headed in the right direction: a life in music felt more possible than ever before.

MY MUSICAL DISCOVERY CONTINUED the next year when my bandmate Alex picked me up from Liaison in his mother's Volvo wagon. When I got in the car, Alex didn't speak, he just pointed at the tape deck. We sat, not driving anywhere, listening to Pixies' debut album *Surfer Rosa*. I looked at Alex, confused, as if tasting beer for the first time: *I think I like this . . . right?* I wanted badly to run in and grab Jared, but he no longer worked there. If he had, I would have bragged about listening to something so exciting, so new and disturbing that I didn't yet possess the vocabulary to articulately define what it was.

Every time the drummer hit the snare it sounded like the speakers might crack. The guitars sounded harsh and abrasive in the best way—like I was sitting in front of the amps. The cover—which was an old-timey black-and-white photo of a topless woman—made no sense to me. A man sang most of the songs and he sounded frustrated. I'd heard plenty of anger in my growing music library—but Pixies' singer was more unhinged and unpredictable. His voice arrested me—it scared me. A woman sang one song, "Gigantic," which was the most memorable and head-bouncing song on the tape. As much as we wanted to scream the frustrated male lyrics, when Alex and I saw each other later that week at a party, our brains both went to the obvious, singsongy "Gigantic." We did our best to imitate bassist Kim Deal, shouting her lyrics, "A big, big love! A big, big love!" over and over. Nobody else knew the song and for that reason, we sang louder, buzzing on the curiosity of those around us. Pixies was *our* band.

Beginning with that colorful Casablanca logo on my Kiss album all those years ago, I had begun to notice logos on the back covers and center labels of records. Other albums in my mother's and uncle's collections had Motown, Impulse!, and Epic logos. Each time I studied the Pixies tape, my eyes returned to the small 4AD logo, which I assumed to be the record label. It looked understated in its rectangular box, and the simple, stately text, "Made in England," told me that 4AD and Pixies were from England, which felt very far away. I didn't realize that although 4AD was a British label, Pixies were from a far less exotic place: Amherst, Massachusetts—the very place where I'd spent four years of my childhood.

MY HIGH SCHOOL YEARS were an especially busy time for new bands coming through Salt Lake City on tour. I'd recently discovered Fishbone, a maniacal band from LA whom many wrote off as ska, but I saw as an exciting new hybrid of funk, punk, and metal. The first time I saw them in Salt Lake City was at the Speedway Cafe, a shitty three-hundred-capacity punk club that was literally on the other side of the tracks. I'd never seen so many Black people at a show in Salt Lake. I assumed it was because all of the many members of Fishbone were Black. For the first time in my life, I recognized that I was getting, and giving, simple nods—subtle gestures of acknowledgment from other Black people.

I wondered what other shows and events I'd been missing. I'd seen the legendary drummer Elvin Jones recently, but at a high-end jazz club full of white people. Later at a show by another Black rock band—Living Colour—the nods with Black people happened again. At first I was hesitant—afraid that they might view me as less Black. But when that didn't seem to happen, I stepped it up, snapping my neck more quickly and maintaining eye contact. I found myself experimenting for the first time—code switching—giving assertive nods to those who were willing to reciprocate, which was everyone. My white friends were oblivious, but I wondered whether they also gave secret signals to other white people. I felt like part of an exclusive club that would disappear when the show ended, and these Black people—who all told made up about 1.5 percent of Salt Lake City's population—were scattered around the city like isolated anomalies.

15.

When Problems Arise

I n Salt Lake City, I learned to be fluid in my race. I could be whoever I wanted to be, whoever people wanted or needed me to be. People could rarely guess my ethnicity but they often asked . . . or stared. When I was at the Living Colour or Fishbone concert, I was Black. But when I was with my friends at a movie or a football game, I was white, like them.

Or maybe I was simply a question mark?

"WE NEED SOME GUYS like you who can run, *Naa*-bill." I'd been in Coach Jensen's weightlifting class since freshman year, and he still couldn't pronounce my name. I was sitting in his office with Andre, the Black quarterback of the football team. The moment I entered the room, I knew Coach wanted to pull me from the cross-country team, whose season ran concurrently with football.

"If you like to run, you can run track in the spring. We want you on the football team with us in the fall."

I didn't really know Andre, but I knew that he wasn't a meat-head jock. He was a bright, sweet kid who happened to play football. Andre explained to me that being on the team had given him the discipline to excel in school. His eyes were apologetic as he spoke.

I listened respectfully, all the time thinking, *I can't believe Andre and I have to sit through this.* I had actual friends on the football team, but Coach Jensen thought it would be more compelling to bring in the one Black kid, with whom he assumed I'd identify, and that I'd quickly trade in my running shoes for a football helmet.

Two things became clear in our short meeting: Coach Jensen saw me as Black, and the stereotyping and tokenization of Black athletes were very real. I was angry but I also felt despair. Even though I hadn't encountered much racial discrimination, I couldn't completely avoid it.

I lied and told Coach Jensen that I'd think about it. But I didn't need to. I was completely disinterested in putting on pads and a helmet and running away from guys who were bigger than me—whose job it was to tackle me to the ground. And I was now against doing anything that would help Coach Jensen, whom I continued to see five mornings a week in class, but after that encounter, I avoided eye contact.

. . .

EAST HIGH SCHOOL HELD SEVERAL formal dances each year.
From homecoming in the fall to senior prom in the spring, every
event was open to the full student body, regardless of grade. I
didn't have a girlfriend, but that didn't matter. Large groups of
friends went together, using the occasion as an excuse to get some
money from our parents, rent a downtown hotel suite, and fill it
with alcohol bought by someone's older brother. We'd attend the
dance itself for only a few minutes, long enough to get an official
photo taken and to find out where others would be partying
later.

I always felt accepted and included, part of the community
that was my school. But deep down, I sometimes wondered where
or when that feeling might change—where a line might exist.
Dating someone's white teenage daughter, to me, was an obvious
potential place for that line to appear.

Anytime a girl said yes to going out with me, I felt relieved.
But then I'd start to think, *Did she tell her parents who she's
going to prom with? What questions did they ask when she said
my name? How many times did she have to repeat it, and was
there a conversation after that?*

The anxiety continued up through the night of the dances.
Each time I walked up to my date's home in my slightly too-large
suit topped with a nervous braces-filled grin, I wondered what
questions her parents would ask me. *What does your father do
for a living? What church do you attend? Where are you from?* I
pictured their faces turning from smiles to friendly confusion as

they asked their daughter to meet them in the kitchen for a moment. I'd imagine the mother emerging to say, "Julie is suddenly not feeling well. I'm so sorry."

These thoughts went through my head every time. And every time I was proved wrong. Not once did I feel that any parent was even a little bit skeptical. Not once did anyone's little sibling blurt out, "He's Black!" Not once did a parent ever mispronounce my name and give me anything less than a firm handshake and a pat on the shoulder. While I was experiencing some racial microaggressions in high school, the situation that worried me the most—dating—proved to be far less complicated. But no matter how many of my dates went without incident, I wasted a significant amount of energy preparing for the one that wouldn't.

In high school, I began to feel like I'd successfully infiltrated Salt Lake City—like I was some sort of undercover operative. Even though my now shorter Afro still stood out, I dressed just like everyone else in my North Face jacket and Polo shirt. My name was still unfamiliar and difficult to pronounce, but I accepted nicknames like "Nibs" and "Nibby," which felt closer to my friends' more common names. Even though I was raised Baha'i, I attended sleepover parties and camping trips with my Mormon friends' families, and occasionally attended church services with them. But I constantly knew I was hiding my real self. Even though I didn't totally know who my real self was.

I was fitting in. But I never took my trusted status for granted. Looking back, I didn't realize at the time how much effort I expended just to prove that I belonged, to continue that sense of subterfuge. When I met a new teacher or a friend's parent for the first time, I'd name-drop the big company my mother worked for, or I'd mention my recent afternoon at the Fort Douglas Country Club, where I wasn't a member but some of my friends were. Statements like these always brought a smile or a raised eyebrow, indicating that people felt more comfortable in my presence. When I entered a nice clothing store, I'd smile and say, "Hey, how's it going," to demonstrate to the clerk that I didn't speak the way they might expect me to; I wasn't the Black kid who was going to steal from them. Once I got my driver's license, I *always* kept it on me, even if I was out for a run. I still do, just in case I need to prove to the police that I'm not the Black man they're looking for. Some of my racial fluidity came naturally, but some was my own doing—always subconsciously auditioning for the part that my friends had inherited automatically.

MY MOTHER AND I REMAINED close during this time, which, based on my friends' families, wasn't par for the course. I put my mother through a lot in high school, and when I look back, I'm shocked at how lucky I was that I never got hurt or into serious trouble.

Twice I was picked up by the police for underage drinking. The first time my mother was worried sick, but the second time she was just angry. My sophomore year was the worst academic year of my life—with a 2.2 grade point average. When my mother went to parent-teacher conferences, she reported back to me that my teachers unanimously cited me as a smart, sometimes even gifted student who was lazy and uninterested in doing anything more than the bare minimum.

My teachers were right. I was uninterested in the academic part of school and completely engulfed in the social scene. I wanted to hang out with friends, go to concerts, play music, drink beer, and occasionally smoke pot. But I was never a bad kid. The vice principal once told my mother, "Nabil is running with a fast crowd, but I'm not worried about him." I have no idea what gave him the ability to see that I was in a different place from many of my friends and to trust that I wouldn't get into serious trouble by being so close to so many flames, but my mother agreed.

I never directly disobeyed my mother, who was far less experienced than many of the parents surrounding us in Salt Lake. I ate dinner at home most nights, sometimes cooking with my mother and sometimes cooking for her. We went to the movies, but to my mother's great disappointment, I would no longer be seen with her at a concert.

Some of our most rewarding time together was spent in the car, in which we would explore the city while listening to music. We'd drive slowly up and down the opulent, tree-lined blocks of Harvard and Yale Avenues, and I'd point out the homes in which I knew the residents. We'd drive to the top of the affluent High Avenues, where we could view the entire Salt Lake Valley at sunset. I'd explain—as an opinionated, fickle teenager—that Descendents was no longer the best band. It was now Jane's Addiction.

I'd blast the tape and my mother would agree, no matter what. Then she'd ask, nervously, probably hoping I'd relent and go with her to a concert, "Are they coming to Salt Lake?"

My mother had left American Express, and now worked for Fidelity Investments, but when Fidelity laid her off, she was unemployed for two months—a long, trying time for a single mother and her teenage son who still wanted to order food delivery, go to concerts, and attend school dances. I was never aware of my friends' financial situations, but most of them had two parents and typically one of those parents was a doctor, lawyer, or banker. I assumed that they were invincible—that no sudden hardship would change their lifestyle. Our lifestyle, though, felt suddenly under threat.

As invincible as my friends' financial security appeared, their personal situations weren't always easy. Friends told me that their mothers considered their fathers lazy and that their fathers considered their mothers too dependent. I watched mothers roll their eyes when fathers spoke, and sometimes that erupted into fights. Those variables didn't exist with my mother and me. We were the entire family. I was always proudly aware that my mother carried the full burden. And I helped out when I could.

When I was sixteen, my mother needed my help for the first time in her life, and it terrified me. She'd walked outside in the dark to drive to the grocery store, and had tripped, falling face-first into the car door frame. When she came back inside, with her hand over the puffy, bleeding gash on her cheek, I instinctively jumped into crisis mode. I set aside my emotions and all fear that my mother could be seriously injured, and I forced her to remove her hand so I could see the wound.

It's not easy for a teenage boy to watch his mother's face bleed. *She can't take care of this. I have to*, I thought as I asked her if I needed to call an ambulance or if I could drive her to the hospital. "I know where it is," I distinctly remember saying. I could sense her worrying less once she realized she wasn't alone in this horrible situation. I drove us to the emergency room, where doctors confirmed that my mother would be fine and that I'd done the right thing bringing her in.

When we got back home, I sunk into the couch. There was a dark knot in my stomach, my head throbbed, and I could hear my heart beating. I closed my eyes, taking several deep breaths, and only then did I feel the delayed wave of love, of terror, of helplessness. What if my mother had been more seriously injured, or worse? I had never before realized how quickly life can change, and that I needed to create as many good memories as I could when I could. I was exhausted—physically and emotionally—but thankful I still had my mom.

16.

Summertime Rolls

I spent less time in New York once I was in high school. I had a solid group of friends in Salt Lake, and my life was no longer based upon the things I missed about New York City—it was more about the things I loved about Salt Lake. As my sophomore year came to a close, I considered for the first time not visiting New York that summer in favor of getting a real job in Salt Lake and earning money. Alan respected my choice but quickly countered with a job offer. His friend Benny shared an office with an attorney in New York City who needed a runner. Minimum wage was $3.35 per hour in Salt Lake, but I was offered $5.00 an hour, cash, in New York City. The choice was easy, and I spent my final two high school summers living with Alan and Shannon in their spacious Chelsea loft.

New York had changed a lot in the five years since we'd moved away, as had Alan's life. He and Shannon now lived in a bustling, hip neighborhood that was more mature than the New York I remembered. The kids who lived nearby carried a palpable swagger—an ownership of their space. They seemed to be clumped together by race, as if someone had stood them against a wall and then separated them into groups based on skin color and hairstyle. The Black kids all wore Afros—not huge seventies Afros but new, shorter, well-kept ones that made me feel self-conscious for having mine cut even shorter. The Puerto Rican kids seemed more bold as they walked in front of moving cars and flashed threatening glares at any driver who dared to honk. The white kids seemed the least aware of their surroundings—caught up in their own small world, preoccupied and tuned out in a way that predated handheld devices.

I had nothing in common with any of the kids in Alan's neighborhood, and I felt intimidated by all of them. Though I'd always navigated my racial identity easily, these groups of teens demonstrated in real life, for the first time, what it might have felt like if I'd had to *choose* a race, if I had to pick a particular pack with which to assimilate. The thought terrified me, and every time I saw the different packs, I looked down and waited for them to pass, hoping nobody would notice me and say something like "What are you?" Or test me by shouting something in Spanish that I didn't understand.

I never made a friend my age during my New York teenage summers.

Instead, I spent most of my days running contracts and documents from office to office. When I wasn't on the streets, getting to know new neighborhoods, I sat at the front desk answering the phone and welcoming visitors. I overheard the attorney scream-ing into the phone about someone who'd wronged a client and how he was going to "ruin her life." I connected calls from celeb-rity musicians and authors. When it was really quiet, I proofread the self-pitying memoir of the attorney's wife, in which every paragraph seemed to end with *How could this happen to me?*

I got to know doormen at the most prestigious office build-ings in the city, so eventually I was able to skip the sign-in line, instead ushered in with a nod. I rode elevators that shot me up fifty stories in seconds, reminding me of my childhood visits to the World Trade Center. When it was urgent, I jumped in front of taxis with my arm held confidently in the air, and I got to know that despite the distance, sometimes the subway was faster . . . and sometimes walking or running was even faster than the sub-way. The capitalist New York City of the late eighties felt alive, pulsing, and lightning fast.

It was during these summers that I began to notice a financial disparity between races. As a child in Amherst, everyone of every race had the same amount of money—very little. In Salt Lake City, most people were white, but even those who weren't were at least middle class. People with less money existed in Salt Lake City, but not near where we lived. In the sweltering, tense New York City summers of 1987 and 1988, it was impossible for me not to notice how racially divided the city had become since I'd moved away and how money was the clearest sign of this divide.

During my messenger job afternoons, I was usually the only non-white person in every polished, antiseptic office building elevator. I was now equal in height to the chisel-jawed, dark-suited men and women who brandished heavy-looking watches and expensive haircuts. But I was lanky in my T-shirt and shorts, and though I was often in a hurry, I knew I didn't look as impatient as the jittery businesspeople who focused their eyes on the ever-changing floor indicator, willing it to move faster to their floor. When non-white people stood in the elevator, they—like me—invariably carried important documents for the white, suited people.

On the streets, Black and Brown people drove the dirty trucks that coughed out puffs of thick gray exhaust. They stood outside in the unbearable heat, placing hot dogs in buns for anxious men and women who had money in their hands even before they reached the brief solace of the hot dog stand's umbrella. They drilled into the city's volatile core with machine-gun-like tools that shook the sidewalk I walked on. They waved their arms and confidently directed traffic with powerful whistle blows. They held doors open with quiet, complacent, glued-on grins. All of this, I thought, the Black and Brown people did in order to keep the city running for the white people.

TV shows and movies of the time, like *Diff'rent Strokes* and *Trading Places*, reinforced my experiences and observations: white people ran things, especially business in New York City. Black and Brown people existed on the periphery as a support system for perpetuating the status quo. A few fortunate ones got in, and when they did, it seemed unusual and outlandish, a happy accident waiting to correct itself.

I'd see these dynamics play out day to day on my job. Upstairs, whenever I got out of an elevator, I'd be in a different world. I'd sit in a spacious lobby after assuring a frustrated secretary that I could not accept her signature, only that of the person whose name appeared on my envelope. On the hottest days of the year, I'd calmly wait, in shorts and a T-shirt stained with sweat with an empty water glass in front of me, on leather couches with $3,000 coffee tables, for a white man in his fifties to come out. When he appeared, he'd be wearing a dark blue or dark gray suit and look freshly showered, unaffected by the oppressive heat outside. His hair would be slicked back, often a color that looked kind of silver but also kind of black, and he'd smell like something expensive. The man always had his own nice pen already in his hand. He'd never say "Hi" or "How are you?" only "Where do I sign?" He never met my eye. And he never needed to do a squiggle on my envelope to get the ink flowing. The pen always worked.

I began to study my unusual window into both worlds—to pay attention to the stark, palpable differences between the lives of the two groups with which I interacted each day. I didn't aspire to belong to either group, but I questioned how and where I fit in.

I perceived the people upstairs to be driven completely by money and power. But very few of them looked happy or fulfilled. On the contrary, they seemed to glow with a desperation and sadness that was sometimes greater than that of the hardworking people on the street.

But the world of the street—where I was a brown person running papers for white people—was a world in which I didn't feel I belonged either. I loved my job, but I knew my paid daily tour of New York City would soon end, and I would return to my utopian bubble in Salt Lake. I'd go to college and eventually end up playing in a band or working for a record company. Or maybe both.

Yes, I was ambitious and I wanted money to buy CDs, clothes, and drums. But I also knew that I never wanted to become the kind of person who would grab a document from someone without acknowledging that there's a hand holding those papers and it belongs to another human being. I was sixteen, and my place as a messenger wasn't to strike up conversations or to call others out for not doing so. But from my many brief interactions I learned a lot about behaviors I never wanted to adopt.

DURING THOSE SUMMERS, whenever I had a free moment between messenger jobs, I was in my favorite musical instrument stores. I noticed new products every time, even if I'd been in the week before. For the first time in my life, I experienced a specific, enviable feeling, the feeling of being paid while being able to stand in one of my favorite places in my favorite city while incoherent musical blasts competed for my attention.

With these moments came thoughts of my father. I rarely

thought about him in Salt Lake City, where there was no sign of him. But in New York City, it was hard to ignore the places that had become inextricably tied to him.

Every time I walked down the stairs to leave Manny's Music, I'd think, *This was the last place I saw him.*

When I passed by a famous club like the Bottom Line or the Blue Note, I visualized my father inside, setting up for a show that night, surrounded by beautiful and talented hangers-on and too busy to say hi to me if I popped my head in.

When I passed by Electric Lady recording studios, I remembered the time Alan and I spent a few awkward minutes at my father's session, and wondered whether he might be inside.

If I ever ran into my father, would either of us recognize each other? If I saw someone who I was positive was him, would I approach him? Or would I let it go in order to save myself the humiliation of not being recognized or a brief, hurried encounter? There was always the chance that I'd catch him at the perfect time—when he was available and interested, even if only for a few minutes.

At the end of those summers, I was always sad to leave New York City, but there was also a relief in returning to Salt Lake City, where I never had to confront the thoughts or memories that involved my father, where I had a new life, completely disconnected from him.

17.

Ayers

It wasn't that I found high school to be difficult, I was just uninterested. But I knew that I'd eventually have to buckle down in order to get into a good college—something I'd always assumed I'd do. I told my orthodontist that I was applying to colleges just before he fixed my mouth open with an imposing metal device. As I sat, only able to make grunts of affirmation or disagreement, Dr. Newton lectured me on the importance of college. One line stuck with me: "Even if you're going to be a bricklayer, it's important to go to college." At the time I had no way of knowing how right he was—that college would offer another level of socialization among smart, motivated people, and greater opportunities to explore my own interests beyond the classroom.

My mother, thankfully, had been very pushy and involved in

the process, taking me on two different trips during my junior year to look at colleges. One to the Northwest to visit several small, expensive liberal arts schools in Washington and Oregon. And a similar trip to Southern California. The West Coast was a popular destination for Salt Lake City kids, and the University of Utah was always an option as well.

I actually used my poor sophomore year grades as the thesis of my college application essay, writing about how much I'd moved as a child and what a shock it had been to move from New York City to Salt Lake City. I wrote about how I'd finally adjusted and that my improved junior year grades were an example of what I'd overcome.

The private universities I considered cost more than we could afford—around $18,000 per year. But my mother assured me that with financial aid, help from Alan and Shannon, and help from the long list of people who had already been influential in my life, we'd figure it out.

I did one-on-one interviews with admissions counselors from several colleges, during which I was not at all blind to what they were likely thinking: *Our school is mostly white. This kid looks different and has a different name.* I got into every school I applied to, most of which were slightly but not terribly out of my league. I attribute my acceptance to three factors: my essay; my interviews, which all went great; and the box I'd ticked on every application—African American.

I remember the conversation with my mother when she calmly stated that no matter how I felt about my identity, checking that box—which I could do truthfully—would help give me a brighter future. I was aware of affirmative action, and I agreed with it in principle. But I never considered that it could benefit *me*. There was a part of me that felt like it was cheating. That I wasn't *fully* Black. Blood aside, I'd assimilated into Salt Lake City, where I knew one or two Black kids in school. I didn't feel white, but I didn't feel Black either. I didn't feel any single race enough to choose only one, and I wanted to tick two boxes, which wasn't an option. In the end, I did what I knew would help the most. I'll always wonder what would have happened if I'd ticked another box.

TOWARD THE END OF high school, my mother suggested that I change my last name. Her parents were Bert and Jean Braufman, and I'd always gone by Braufman, which goes back generations to the Romanian name Braufmanu. My mother had used the last name Braufman until she started working in human resources at Fidelity Investments. In her role there, she conducted hundreds of interviews, some of which were exit interviews after an employee was let go. A few weeks of this had brought back her New York City street smarts, causing her to change her last name to Blair. It wasn't a legal name change, but she used it at work to protect her privacy.

She was shocked at how much easier it made her life. Never spelling Braufman: "*B* as in 'boy,' *R*, *A*, *U*, *F* as in Frank . . ." It always took forever, and people still got it wrong.

I didn't want to make up a name or pick one out of thin air like my mother had, so only one name made sense. Ayers.

Whether or not I felt a connection to my father, it was his name, which made the connection inherent. I liked that it was five letters, like my first name and my middle name, Amahl. Little did I know at the time that—coupled with a younger generation of musicians and fans discovering my father's music and his continued world touring—I'd chosen a name that would identify me as my father's son, seemingly forever.

On a sunny summer afternoon in 1989, my mother and I went to the Salt Lake City courthouse and filed the papers to legally change my last name. I'd make a clean break, using Ayers for the first time at the University of Puget Sound, the college I was about to start, nine hundred miles from home, in Tacoma, Washington.

18.

The Real Thing

Nirvana's debut album *Bleach* was released in June 1989. Three months later, during my first week of college, Soundgarden released their second album, *Louder Than Love*. And that November, Mudhoney's self-titled debut arrived. "Grunge," I quickly learned, was a real thing, and bands from Seattle were playing powerful, heavy, sweaty music at exceptionally high volumes and rebelliously slow speeds.

I'd chosen a college in the Northwest for a few reasons: I wanted to leave Salt Lake for a bigger city; I didn't like California, which felt fun to visit but too one-dimensional to call home; and I wanted to be closer to music—to see, listen to, and play as much as I could. Seattle simply felt musical, with record stores and venues everywhere.

When I arrived at the University of Puget Sound, my life quickly flipped upside down in the best possible way. Instead of knowing more about music than everyone else, kids from other cities now told me about bands I'd never heard of. We sat around dimly lit dorm rooms, taking turns on cassette and CD players while trying to mask the smell of harsh joints and cheap beer. On weekends, my new friends were always willing to drive forty-five minutes to Seattle to see a band and shop at any of a dozen great record stores.

My high school friends who'd chosen colleges in California and Arizona told stories of heroic outdoor parties with fake palm trees, trucked-in sand, and live reggae bands. Meanwhile, thanks to the constant rain, I was stuck inside, but I had my friends and my music, whose origin suddenly made complete sense. As my first semester drew to a close, it never poured, but it drizzled constantly, and darkness set in daily around 4:00 p.m. These sludgy, dark, heavy sounds got me through my first otherwise depressing fall in the Northwest.

THE UNIVERSITY OF PUGET SOUND was nestled in a scenic enclave of the otherwise working-class and gang-ridden city of Tacoma. When I attended, UPS was a collection of 2,800 students who were mostly white and affluent and in our own little world. We were in college, living away from home for the first time. But we were doing so in a protected bubble a short walk from an ethnically diverse and economically depressed city. It was easy to rarely leave campus and remain closed off from the real world that existed just outside.

Amid my voracious musical discovery and my love of living away from home, I was a seventeen-year-old college freshman who still hated to study. I had convinced myself that in the right environment—a small college more like my experimental grade schools in Amherst and New York City—I'd thrive in intimate classes with eager, intellectual peers and creative, genius professors. While that was the liberal arts education I'd expected, my freshman year consisted mostly of large classes in lecture halls and weekly exams that I was expected to pass by reading, listening, taking notes, and memorizing. Academically, college felt like a more challenging high school, one in which I was among its least motivated students. *Everyone* else at UPS seemed as smart as or smarter than everyone I'd known in high school, and they'd all come from different backgrounds—though mostly white—with different points of view.

Over the course of my four-and-a-half years at UPS, I barely hung on academically. But I excelled in other ways, playing music, putting on shows and parties, and getting involved in student government. I'd brought my guitar with me to college but not my drum set. I played drums whenever I could—jamming with friends at parties—but I played guitar every day, and it quickly became my primary instrument.

Tons of kids at UPS played music, and it was easy to connect with them in the close quarters of my freshman dorm. Both of my roommates were musicians. Jon was a tall, quiet academic from nearby Kent, Washington, who played trombone. Luke was an energetic premed student who had grown up in Eureka, California, where he played trumpet in Mr. Bungle, the band Mike Patton left (and eventually returned to) to join Faith No More just before they recorded their breakthrough album *The Real Thing*.

I shared a weekly radio show with my friend Jason Livermore, a handsome jock who was on a swimming scholarship. Jason was a drummer who'd lived outside of Berkeley, California, and had seen punk shows at the legendary venue 924 Gilman Street. We knew that nobody listened to our show on KUPS, but we used our two-hour shift to rapaciously explore the station's music library and educate ourselves. We read the weekly trade magazine *College Music Journal* cover to cover, and other times, we simply pulled CDs off the shelf and played them because they had a cool cover, or because they had Sub Pop or Matador or 4AD logos printed on the spine. Pixies released three albums between 1989 and 1991, and we played them weekly, without fail.

One weekend, my friend Dane and I jumped in his car with no plan other than to drive 150 miles south to Portland, Oregon, to see R.E.M. play. We arrived the afternoon of the show, and while at a red light, we saw Henry Weinhard's brewery. The FREE BREWERY TOURS sign spoke to us, saying, *You two underage college freshmen should come in and try to drink free beer!*

When we entered, the old building smelled of wet hops and freshly cleaned floors. Our guide opened his hand toward two stools at the empty tasting bar. We accepted his invitation—both of us trying to hide our excitement—and greeted the bartender, a stocky man in his thirties with an obvious East Coast accent.

"I've only lived out here for a year," he told us without being asked, as we received our first round of free beers. "It's different out west. You don't see these things where I'm from . . . these salt-and-pepper couples." He pointed outside, as if a racially mixed couple were walking past us exactly then. I just sipped my beer, a seventeen-year-old salt-and-pepper boy with his white friend, il-legally drinking beer served by an old-school racist. *Obviously he can't tell my race*, I thought, or *he wouldn't say something like that in front of me.* His comment made me wonder—in my seven-teen years, how many times had someone wanted to make a racist comment but held it back because they thought they might offend me personally? I almost never heard racist comments in Salt Lake, but maybe it happened all the time when I wasn't present.

FORTY PERCENT OF UPS STUDENTS were fraternity or soror-ity members. My childhood photos weren't of me on boats or ski slopes, they were of a hippie kid with an Afro, wearing raggedy clothes and holding a pair of drumsticks on an urban sidewalk— a very happy kid, but one who didn't fit the fraternity mold. But I was curious enough to give UPS's fraternity system the benefit of the doubt.

My freshman friends and I went through rush, the very orga-nized process in which prospective fraternity members visit each house and meet its members. Over the course of four days, each rushee spends an increasing amount of time at a decreasing num-ber of houses, based on a mutual ranking system. I'd met a lot of people whom I really liked—people from Salt Lake, people who liked the same bands I did and had other shared interests. And they seemed to like me. Nobody asked the questions I feared: *What does your father do? What kind of car do you drive? What race are you?*

Still, I wasn't entirely comfortable. There's a scene in the movie *Animal House* in which some non-white men are rushing. They're treated well on the surface—greeted with smiles and firm handshakes, but then they're pawned off on the least desirable members of the fraternity. *Was I that guy?* It was the members' job to make everyone feel welcome, but was I truly welcome? I feared that my race and socioeconomic background made me a prime candidate to be, at best, uninvited to join a fraternity or, at worst, humiliated during the process of trying.

On the final day of rush, I was asked back by my top two fraternity choices. But my second choice scared me. The guys were tightly wound and had stereotypical fraternity nicknames like Puddles and Chainsaw. The blond, buttoned-up, chisel-jawed house president could never pronounce my name correctly. Happily, I accepted an offer from my first choice along with two dozen other freshmen.

Should I be in this fraternity? I sometimes thought after I joined. Sigma Alpha Epsilon fraternity was founded in 1856 in Tuscaloosa, Alabama. All eight of its founding fathers fought for the Confederacy in the Civil War. But more often I thought it was important to be there, among a relatively mixed group of people—some of whom were Jewish, Hispanic, Indian, Black, Japanese, and gay—helping the system to evolve, rather than rejecting it based on its history.

While I made strides in the fraternity, I opted not to join another more obvious organization. Every semester in college, I received a call from the Black Student Union asking me to come to a meeting. I always politely declined, feeling that I wasn't Black enough and that, paradoxically, my traditionally white fraternity offered more diversity than the exclusive BSU. Nonetheless, the call came twice a year because my name was on a short list of UPS students who'd ticked the African American box on our applications.

I imagined the Black Student Union to have meetings where a dozen Black students criticized the university's lack of diversity and specifically called out the fraternity system for its perceived inherent racism. If I went, I thought, the members of my fraternity would have been fine with it. But I also thought the BSU membership wouldn't have been fine with my fraternity association. Though completely made up, my line of thinking caused me to never attend a BSU meeting, and in retrospect, I wish I had. That's the only way I'd have truly learned what it was like.

AT UPS, I EASILY FIT IN. My exotic name, my light but not white skin, and my Afro were all assets that made me appealing. But that didn't mean it was easy for me internally, constantly wondering if, given the opportunity, one of my friends would expose themselves as a racist, or if one of my professors would somehow try to exploit my racial background, like Coach Jensen had in high school.

In college, kids occasionally told stories that included lines like "so this big Black guy walks in" or "and suddenly these three Black guys show up." I quickly realized that the term "Black guy" was meant to create dramatic effect, to make the listener understand a perceived threat—big, angry, imposing. When the term was used, the listener knew that something was about to change; the power and control in the story had suddenly shifted. I was always worried that a story would descend into a more racist one, replete with slurs and stereotypes. It never did, but I couldn't ignore the tension I felt anytime the term was used.

Once I tried using it myself. I mentioned "a big Black bouncer" at the door of a club, and I paused to gauge my friends' reactions. They all gave a knowing nod, as if I'd just said something relatable. I'd successfully escalated my story, but I felt horrible, like I'd just given my friends a test and they'd all failed. Nobody said, "Why does it matter that the bouncer is Black?" It reminded me of the time my childhood friend Michael recited his little racist poem. But unlike my interaction with Michael, I never questioned my college friends out loud.

Most of them had grown up in cities larger and more cosmopolitan than Salt Lake, like Portland, Seattle, or San Francisco. But because their cities and high schools were more diverse, I learned, their social groups were more segregated. In Salt Lake, everyone had hung out together. But in the larger, diverse high schools that my college friends had attended, members of each race tended to naturally clump together.

This meant that in college, I was a lot of my white friends' "first Black friend." And that came with its own challenges. At parties, where early nineties hip-hop dictated that white kids danced their asses off, I distinctly recall my friends always physically making room for me—in the form of a compliment—as if I were expected to demonstrate *how it was really done*. But I've never liked to dance. I was disappointed anytime anyone attributed my drumming skills to my racial background. And whenever I explained my racial background, I could see people's brains churn. I imagined them thinking new things: that my father was Harry Belafonte or Miles Davis—someone much more famous than my actual father—someone they'd heard of. I imagined that even though I'd just told them I was half-white and half-Black, they'd still be stuck on my name, wondering if I was secretly the heir to an oil fortune in the Middle East—a lineage that at the time, just before and during the Gulf War, carried a lot of clout.

I've mostly blocked out—either mentally or because of too many shots of stinging, plastic-bottled tequila—the Crips & Bloods party, at which dozens of white fraternity and sorority members wore blue and red bandannas, and plaid shirts with only the top button buttoned, and flashed faux gang signs. Meanwhile, real Crips and Bloods routinely shot each other just two miles away in downtown Tacoma.

GROWING UP IN SALT LAKE, I told people that my parents were divorced. It was always the easiest explanation because it was familiar to people and required no further conversation. But in college, I eventually realized I was doing a huge disservice to my mother and to the amazing job she did raising me, without any support—financial or otherwise—from my father.

It wasn't easy to tell the truth about my childhood without either giving a long explanation or leaving people to draw their own incorrect conclusions. But being honest made it easier to explain that we didn't view my father as a deadbeat dad because he didn't send us child support. We weren't on the short end of a bad situation. We were in the situation my mother created, the one my father agreed to. And it was okay.

The film *Six Degrees of Separation* came out in 1993, the year I graduated from college. It stars a college-aged Will Smith, whose character Paul Poitier feigns injury to stumble into the upscale apartment owned by the white parents of his supposed boarding school friend. The parents immediately take him in and, believing that he is the son of actor Sidney Poitier, spend the night enraptured with the boy and his eloquent tales. Smith's character, though, turns out to be an imposter—a con man who has carefully researched and made up his entire story.

I saw the film soon after graduating from college, and I really resonated with the character of Paul Poitier. I'd also come from nothing and ended up in a fancy, selective college. I'd also spent weekends and holidays with friends whose last names were the same as gigantic corporations I'd known my entire life. At dining tables larger than any bedroom I'd ever occupied, I regaled people with stories about my uncle's decrepit loft in New York City, my young single mother, and the Black father I'd never known.

But unlike the movie, it wasn't a con, and the more I talked, the more accepted I felt. I was not an imposter; in fact, at twenty-one, I had the most interesting, authentic experience of anyone in the room.

19.

Nevermind

About halfway through college, my mother started to talk about Jim, a wonderful man she'd met while attending a work conference in San Antonio, Texas. Jim was a lawyer from Berkeley, California, whom she'd run into in the dinner buffet line. Both complaining that there weren't enough vegetarian options, they began to chat, and instead of settling for assembly line sides of mushy broccoli and overly salted potatoes, they strolled around San Antonio and enjoyed a dinner that consisted of French bread and Sprite—the only vegetarian meal they could find that late at night. But they enjoyed it together.

I finally met Jim while I was home for the holidays my junior year. He complemented my mother in many ways—he brought calmness, solitude, and Berkeley Zen to my mother's amped alertness, something that remained even after nearly a decade away from New York City. Jim had only ever lived in Berkeley and the small South Dakota town in which he'd been raised, but he carried a kind, liberal thoughtfulness that reminded me of our friends in Amherst. I immediately liked him. Jim was also a nondrinking vegetarian who liked to run—it was comforting to know that my mother's criteria hadn't changed a bit in over twenty years.

I'd never seen my mother so happy. She'd devoted nearly two decades to me and had never been in a serious relationship during that time. Now I was in college and it was her turn. At the time I was too young to worry about her—I was twenty and she was forty-two. Looking back, I realize Jim took a lot of pressure off me. My mother wasn't any less attentive or doting—I knew that would never change—and suddenly she had her own life with someone she loved and cared about deeply.

Less than a year after they met, my mother moved to Berkeley to live with Jim. Their house was perfect: a small, tidy, two-bedroom Spanish villa in a cozy cul-de-sac. They were close to San Francisco and Oakland, but their home felt secluded. It reminded me of Amherst, Greenwich Village, and Salt Lake City all at once, and I knew it was home when I smelled the kitchen, which had the light but permanent smell of salty soy sauce and earthy brown rice.

Not long after my first visit, I flew back to Berkeley for my mother and Jim's small wedding of about twenty guests in their backyard. Following Baha'i tradition, they wrote their own vows, and their wedding was witnessed by a Berkeley Baha'i assembly member. My uncle Alan was the only other family—my grand-parents were too old to make the trip from Long Island—but several longtime friends of my mother's from Salt Lake City were in attendance, creating a warm, intimate event.

At the wedding, I started to think about my father in a different way than I ever had before. I wished he could be there for just a few minutes to see how happy we were, to see how well we were both doing. He'd have seen a woman glowing with calm happiness. And he'd see her proud son, about to graduate from a prestigious college, whose only care in the world was what to do with his life, which sounded grand but actually wasn't. I had family and friends who loved me and looked out for me. And even though I didn't have it figured out, I felt closer to music and the music business than ever before. I knew my life was full of options.

I'D BEEN CLOSE with the same college buddies for two years, so in retrospect, I'm not sure why it took my friend Jason Livermore and me so long to start a band. We had always made a point to see music together. In 1991, Jason and I walked two hours in the rain from our parking spot to see a show on the first Lolla-palooza tour, with Jane's Addiction, Siouxsie and the Banshees, Violent Femmes, Fishbone, and Ice-T and Body Count. We drove two hours south to Portland instead of to nearby Seattle in order to see Sonic Youth in a smaller, better venue. We sweated in a cramped Seattle record store while Nirvana debuted songs from their not-yet-released album *Nevermind* for a lucky roomful of fans.

In our junior year of college, we finally got our act together and started our band. I played guitar, Jason played drums, my freshman roommate Luke sang and played trumpet and keyboards, and our bespectacled, lacrosse-playing friend Chris played bass. We covered college-friendly party songs by Jane's Addiction, the Red Hot Chili Peppers, and Alice in Chains. And finally, we started writing our own music.

It wasn't easy.

At night, Jason and I continued to see bands—loud, straight-ahead bands like Seaweed and Mudhoney, but we couldn't write music like theirs. On our radio show, we continued to play lazy guitar bands like Sebadoh and Pavement, but we couldn't write music like theirs either. Everyone in our band was technically a good musician, which I later realized might have been a handicap: some of the best bands are great because, while they might not be masters of their instruments, they have something to say. Music is a powerful vessel for a message, especially when its looseness fosters an emotional connection. We, unfortunately, were very tight, and while it was a ton of fun, there was no real passion in what we did.

After a few shows, it became time to name our band. Spontaneous Funk Whorehouse quickly stuck, and although it stands out as one of the worst band names I've ever heard, it did kind of fit our sound, a college band that couldn't decide its focus. Our music leaned toward off-kilter, percussive Bay Area bands like Mr. Bungle and Primus. Our friends called us SFW for short, and those who didn't like us called us So Fucking What. We quickly advanced from college house parties to local Tacoma bars like Magoo's and Cheers West.

Within a few months, we recorded a five-song demo, which took two full days and served as my first time recording in a real studio. I loved the smell of new carpet and the fact that we spent more time meticulously tweaking sounds and mixing the tracks than actually playing. We had an engineer who gave us positive reinforcement but also told us when we should change a part. In the studio, we were a real band. SFW pressed one hundred cassettes and they sold out right away, just like my high school band's cassette. Soon SFW released a CD. We received heavy airplay on the local radio station KGRG, which had a strong signal and real listeners.

I'll never forget the first time I heard myself on the radio and cranked the volume in my friend's car as we turned a corner onto campus. Even though I knew KGRG was a small station, I was famous for those three minutes.

SFW opened for big regional bands like Sweet Water, Blackhappy, and the Cherry Poppin' Daddies—bands who drew five hundred or more people. *Imagine*, we fantasized, *if we could be that big someday.* We played a show in *Seattle*—a major milestone—opening for Critters Buggin at RKCNDY. The club—where we'd seen real bands like Teenage Fanclub and Afghan Whigs—never felt more intimidating than when we arrived that afternoon and were greeted by the unimpressed sound man who actually wore flannel and appeared to be auditioning for a role in Cameron Crowe's grunge film *Singles*.

. . .

WHILE SFW WAS GROWING, I continued trying to move toward music as my full-time job. Every semester, I attempted to get an internship at Sub Pop Records. The Seattle label—which I revered—had released early music by Nirvana, Soundgarden, and Mudhoney. When I didn't receive a response to the résumé I'd diligently embellished and mailed to them, I began to call. When my calls went nowhere, I finally decided I'd stop by their headquarters. That afternoon, my breath felt short as I rode the elevator eleven floors to the label's office, and I worried that my hands were sweating on my freshly folded résumé. When I arrived, the receptionist nicely told me that my résumé was at the top of the pile, but that was as far as I got.

Eventually I gave up on Sub Pop after stumbling into an internship at PolyGram Group Distribution, the largest of the then six major label distribution companies, which included the legendary labels A&M Records, Island Records, and Mercury Records. A friend had seen the posting on campus and told me about it, and though I imagined it would be competitive, PGD didn't have the brand recognition that Sub Pop did, and I was one of very few applicants. A short phone interview landed me the job.

My boss Steph was twenty-six with a punchy voice and red bangs. She'd grown up in Seattle and seemed to know everyone and every band—her husband had played in the early grunge band Mother Love Bone. She blasted music in her beat-up yellow van and treated everyone—even the crankiest record store clerks—

with respect and kindness. For those reasons, I idolized her. Twice a week I drove to her Seattle home office to stuff boxes with CDs and posters that featured PJ Harvey, U2, the Gin Blossoms, and Redd Kross. I mailed packages to record stores, called stores to track sales, and often drove around Seattle to put up posters and deliver promo CDs. I listened in on high-level conference calls, went to lots of shows, and met every PGD artist who came through Seattle. On Sheryl Crow's first promotional tour, Sheryl and I spoke for a few minutes during which I wanted to tell her, "I'm just an intern, go talk to someone more important!"

One afternoon Steph asked me to join her while she completed my intern evaluation from the University of Puget Sound. It was a sunny spring afternoon, and we sat on her front steps drinking beer as Steph rolled through questions that covered everything from my punctuality to my willingness to take on challenges, all of which she answered favorably. But there was one issue she wanted to discuss with me.

"You need to be more forceful with your name," Steph said frankly. "Sometimes you can be too quiet when you introduce yourself." I sunk into myself, knowing she was right. "Say, 'Hi, I'm Nabil.' And if they look confused or don't repeat it back to you, say: 'Nabil. It's an Arabic name. Nabil.' Now you've said it three times." From that point on, I introduced myself with more confidence—and repetition, when necessary. Steph showed me that when presented correctly, my name wasn't a confusing thing I had to explain, it was an asset that served as a great conversation starter.

. . .

IN MY JUNIOR YEAR, I'd been elected social chairman of my fraternity, where I did more than simply plan parties. I handled weekly negotiations with the dean's office to get our alcohol permits signed before the parties. I oversaw a healthy budget. I instituted a system of creative accounting so that sororities could contribute to alcohol purchases for the first time ever—something they were strictly forbidden to do. I hired live bands and brought in fencing companies so we could expand our parties outdoors in the spring. And I listened to and represented one hundred people, many of whom didn't always agree on our party strategy. It was my first real job, and I poured myself into my position, leading to my becoming president my senior year.

The president carried a big title—eminent archon. The title always brought me back to thoughts about the fraternity's early days—it felt all too close to the KKK, who used titles like Grand Dragon and Grand Wizard to describe its leadership. But the thought of me, a Black, white, Baha'i, Jewish son of a single mother becoming eminent archon of a respected chapter of the biggest national fraternity . . . I loved it. Not only had I joined the system, I'd beat it. My goal hadn't been to dismantle it, but to continue to push it forward.

At UPS I created a new student government position, overseeing the new Campus Music Network. There were several bands on campus, and I was given a budget to put on concerts, send each band into a proper recording studio, and release a compilation tape of the recordings. I was thrilled to hear that after I graduated, the program continued to exist and that each year a new compilation had been released on CD. My academic adviser, though disappointed with my poor academic performance for nearly four years, sat me down one day to tell me how impressed he was with the Campus Music Network and that he was submitting me for an award. I explained to him—unapologetically—that contrary to what my transcripts said, I was receiving an excellent education at UPS. I may have majored in communication, but my real classes were deejaying at KUPS, playing in a band, interning at PolyGram, planning parties, and now overseeing the Campus Music Network. That spring, I sat in a roomful of overachieving seniors who I assumed looked down on me on the days that I *did* attend class, and I accepted one of the university's highest honors, the Oxholm Award for Superior Service to the University Community.

20.

Easy Street

A long with many UPS graduates, I moved forty-five minutes north to Seattle after my senior year in the summer of 1993. My friends were in law school and graduate programs, and working for big local companies like Microsoft or Boeing. But I didn't share their postcollege goals. I wanted to be in a touring band, and I knew that any kind of real job would prevent that from happening. And as much as I loved my record company internship and had long-term goals to work in the music business, even that felt far off—secondary to playing drums for a living.

While my friends shopped for suits, moved into nice apartments, and took me to steak dinners on their shiny new corporate credit cards, I worked for a temporary agency, where I earned enough to cover my living expenses and had enough time and energy to let everyone know that I wasn't looking for a job, I was looking for a band.

Steph from PolyGram set me up with a job interview at Easy Street Records, a great record store in the West Seattle Junction, an antiquated, old-American downtown district near the house I shared with Jason and three other roommates. Matt, who owned the store, was surprisingly young—in his twenties—and affable with a quiet confidence. I'd never worked in a record store, but I accidentally nailed the interview when Matt explained to me, "We're not just a cool record store, we sell everything from Metallica to Roy Ayers." I told Matt that Roy was my father, and I started my new job the next day. That was the first time my father had ever done something for me, even if it was unintentional.

Music was more exciting than ever, and I had even more access to it at Easy Street, where the senior staff constantly exposed me to previously unfamiliar artists. I worked alongside Kirsten, a wonderful, pale goth with a black bob who once explained to me the sensuality of menstrual blood while blasting Nick Cave's *Let Love In*. Stephen, the manager who sang in a band that had *almost* been signed and who wore a puffy white shirt under a tight black vest, played the goth band Fields of the Nephilim every day. New CDs arrived daily, and we listened to everything from Portishead's gloomy, haunting debut to *Gling-Gló*, the twenty-four-dollar import-only jazz vocal album by Björk.

West Seattle seemed like a separate city from Seattle, even though it was only a ten-minute drive from downtown. There were some very rough parts—my roommates and I each paid $154 per month for our five-bedroom house near High Point, where there was gang activity. West Seattle also had areas on the water around Alki Beach, where some Seattle rock stars chose to live, removed from the city.

Soundgarden's singer Chris Cornell sometimes arrived at Easy Street right at 9:00 p.m., when we were scheduled to close. He would start shopping as the store was clearing out and nicely ask whoever was working to let him stay just a bit longer so that he could shop in private.

Pearl Jam's singer Eddie Vedder shopped at Easy Street during our regular hours. I was working once when Eddie came in and bought our entire Who section—about fifteen CDs. He wore a tight green ski cap and stood in line, impatiently fidgeting with a childlike grin on his face. The kid in front of him bought a Pearl Jam CD and had no idea who was standing in line behind him— this caused Eddie and me to exchange a knowing smirk. He paid with hundred-dollar bills, then bolted out the door. I watched his green cap bounce down the street until it was out of sight.

My roommates and I often piled into Jason's navy blue Isuzu Trooper to see shows at RKCNDY, the Off Ramp, or one of the many other rock clubs in Seattle. To save money, we learned which bars sold which beers and we filled a cooler in the back of the Trooper that was stocked according to that night's venue. RKCNDY meant Budweiser tall boys. The Crocodile Cafe meant Sierra Nevada pale ale bottles. We made trips to the car to restock our jackets between bands. My cheap rent, Easy Street guest list privileges, and nonexistent bar tabs made for an inexpensive, carefree postcollege life in Seattle.

Because of my experience at PolyGram, Matt gave me the role of label representative at Easy Street. I was responsible for dealing with the various record label representatives who called and visited the store. It was my job to make sure the poster displays were current and relevant, ensure we had in-store play copies of every new release, field phone calls when labels wanted to know how many copies of an album we'd sold, compile and send out the weekly sales charts, and take care of all guest list requests for the staff at upcoming shows.

It was the heyday of the CD, when relatively unknown alternative artists like No Doubt or Alanis Morissette could quickly sell millions of albums. Seattle and Easy Street had become very important in the national picture, and I was right in the middle of it. Suddenly I knew everyone. Label people often called the store from New York and Los Angeles. I spoke to the trade magazines and I was quoted in *CMJ*, *Hits*, and *Album Network*. If I wanted a personal copy of a new album, all I had to do was ask. I met every hot new act from Liz Phair to Veruca Salt to Everclear. I ate and drank for free all the time, and was invited to every show and every party. Though I wasn't playing in a band, Easy Street was a dream job where I could sense my acceleration into the music industry.

21.

Sour Times

I soon fell into a rock band called the Lemons after temporarily filling in for their drummer, who'd broken his arm. The Lemons played sleazy, suburban rock with simple, catchy riffs like the Ramones. (The Lemons were sometimes referred to as the Lamones.) The singer had a glam-ish LA snarl, and the songs were all under three minutes long. My bandmates looked like they were in *Grease* or *Happy Days*: all very pale white, wearing white T-shirts and black leather jackets and sporting dyed black hair. I stood out with my glasses and now mini-dreadlocked Afro, and I thought a lot about how and where I fit in with the Lemons, with whom I had very little in common—not even musical taste. In college, I'd been into dissonant, experimental rock bands like Drive Like Jehu and Jawbox. The Lemons, who were not that, represented a giant step away from where I wanted to be musically.

But I'd never played with such a powerful, straight-ahead rock band, and I found it to be addictive. One heavy, loud guitar amp sat on either side of me in our practice room, and together, we sounded like a hefty, chugging freight train. My bandmates accepted me, and we were united—not by haircuts or clothing—but by our collective desire to *rock*.

I WAS ABOUT TO PLAY my first show with the Lemons, opening for Mudhoney in front of six thousand people at a free outdoor show at the base of Seattle's Space Needle. Mudhoney was one of Seattle's coolest and most respected bands. Just two years earlier I'd stood in line outside Tower Records at midnight to buy their new album *Piece of Cake*—their first after graduating from Sub Pop to Warner Records. Now I was hanging out backstage with Mudhoney, about to play on the same stage as they were.

I hadn't played drums live in a couple of years, and I'd never played for an audience even close to this size. I went all out in the first song, and afterward I felt weak—as if I'd just sprinted for too long. I could actually hear my heartbeat in my head as the guitars continued to ring out and I tried to catch my breath. All three of my bandmates looked at me just like they had in our few cram session practices—not with disappointment but with smiles of approval that told me I'd successfully survived the most difficult part of the set.

The rest of the show was a thirty-minute blur of sharp sunlight and egregious volume during which I learned to pace myself and felt more comfortable with each song—each a three-minute victory. After the show, fans stood in a long line to buy a Lemons CD, and all of them complimented my drumming. In thick black Sharpie pen I sloppily signed each CD *Art*, the name of the former drummer. Once again I felt the great rush that comes from recognition. I thought about it in the context of my father, whom I'd seen thrive in the same setting.

One evening at practice, Jimmy, the Lemons' outspoken singer, started a conversation about my glasses. "I bet I could hook you up with a free pair of Ray-Bans." Jimmy boasted of his friend who worked for the sunglasses company. "If you put regular lenses in them, I bet they'd look really fucking cool." I appreciated his tact. He didn't tell me that my current wire-rim glasses were uncool, preppy, or dorky. Instead, he offered to get me a free new pair of Ray-Bans.

When I wore my new glasses to work, I once again felt like the new kid on my first day at a new school: nervous and apprehensive about what my colleagues would think. But when everyone complimented my thick black frames, I began to feel comfortable. I loved how sturdy they were, unlike every delicate pair I'd ever owned before. That weekend, the Lemons played a show—my first with my new glasses. They were strong, like athletic gear, able to take considerably more abuse. They could withstand the accidental hit of a drumstick and not slip around from large amounts of sweat. After our set, a long-haired Eddie Vedder–like Seattleite approached me. "You look like a pounding, mad professor back there!" He said it with squinting eyes and a nodding head, which told me he was serious. I knew I'd found my new look.

The Lemons were soon courted by several major record labels, something that was still happening at a furious rate in Seattle in the midnineties. We made a few trips to New York and Los Angeles to meet with labels, and when Mercury Records appeared to be the most interested and flew us to New York to meet its newly appointed president, Ed Eckstine, we hoped to close the deal. We'd heard that Ed had come from an R&B background. I knew that Polydor, Mercury's sister label, had released Roy Ayers's albums in the seventies and eighties, and I was positive that Ed—the first-ever Black president of a major US record label—had crossed paths with my father at some point in his career.

In our meeting with Ed, in a plush office high above New York City, I nodded and smiled, but much of the conversation went past me because I was thinking about my father, whom I wanted to bring up but didn't for fear of where the conversation might lead. "Oh, I just got off the phone with him." Or worse: "He's in a meeting downstairs, let's pop in and say hello!" These possibilities felt completely plausible to me, and terrified me so much that when we walked from office to office to meet the staff, I braced myself for a run-in with my father—what would have been my first in thirteen years. I worried he wouldn't recognize me and I'd have to explain to him—in front of all these music executives and my bandmates—who I was. I didn't run into my father that day after all, but the experience made him more present in my mind.

As part of Mercury's courtship, Angie—the A&R person who wanted to sign the Lemons—took us on a shopping spree at Tower Records. At the time, I didn't own any of my father's music on CD, so when I saw Roy Ayers's *Evolution: The Polydor Anthology* positioned above the bin, I tossed it in our collective shopping basket. On the cover, my father stares seductively at the camera, wearing a silken silver robe as he leans on his vibraphone. The two-CD set spans Roy's seventies career, and it turned me on to songs of his that I'd never known, from the funky theme song to the 1973 Pam Grier film *Coffy* to "Africa—Centre of the World," Roy's 1979 collaboration with Fela Kuti, which came together after Roy toured Africa with Fela for three weeks. I'd always thought of Roy as a jazz artist—he played in jazz clubs, and his music was always in the jazz section in record stores. *The Polydor Anthology* gave me a clearer picture of who my father was musically. Though "Everybody Loves the Sunshine" remains my favorite song of his, I learned that he'd spent three decades building a more diverse catalog of music than I'd realized.

WE ULTIMATELY SIGNED WITH Mercury Records, and the Lemons spent three years recording and touring. It was on those tours that I became an adult. Not via sex, drugs, or even rock and roll, but through interpersonal relationships with my bandmates, manager, attorney, label staff, booking agent, and the hundreds of other bands and locals I met, along with our common experiences on the road.

Like all small bands, the Lemons toured in a van. Up until then, I'd felt well traveled for my twenty-three years. I'd driven the nine hundred miles between Salt Lake City and Tacoma a few times on college breaks, and down to Tijuana and back on an epic spring break trip in an RV. But touring America in a van—traversing its endless freeways, sliding uncontrollably across lanes in the Montana snow, driving the full, expansive width of Texas—is how I learned how large this country truly is. Whether for gas, food, or a pee break, the Lemons' van stopped often, and it was on those stops that I became acquainted with America.

Every time we stopped outside of a major city, I looked for anything suspicious before I got out of the van, something my white bandmates never thought to do—something they never *had* to do. When I saw more than one bald head crowded around a muscle car, I asked my bandmates to bring me back a sandwich. When I saw a "Stop White on White Crime" bumper sticker on a jacked-up truck, I knew I had to wait for the next stop for water. And when I saw a dark, thick swastika tattoo on a shirtless chest, I locked the doors and lay down on the van bench, holding in my piss and anxiously awaiting my bandmates' return.

In a rural North Dakota gas station that felt homemade, a grizzly, wild-eyed local approached me and my bandmate and held his dirty-nailed fist inches from our faces. He'd noticed our Washington license plate and stated firmly as his fist shook, "Mount Rainier here doesn't have a sense of humor." His statement didn't make sense, but he said it with enough conviction that we immediately turned and walked away.

In Fort Collins, Colorado, a small pack of baseball-capped, denim-jacketed hicks surrounded me, looked me up and down, and demanded, "What are you?"

Then, in the middle of the Utah desert, we were arrested and charged with felony possession of a controlled substance with intent to distribute—a charge that, because of the large amount of pot we carried, could carry a mandatory prison sentence.

We convinced the small-town judge and the prosecutor that as musicians, our jobs required us to finish our tour. So our preliminary hearing date was scheduled for a date soon after our tour ended. The rest of the tour was brutal: six weeks driving around America as the days darkened and fall turned into winter. We lived in both cheap motels and a freezing, rented Ryder truck because our comfortable van and trailer had been seized as evidence. The same model truck had been used in the Oklahoma City bombing earlier that year, causing us to be pulled over, questioned, and searched daily in Oklahoma and its surrounding states. Felony charges and prison time hung over our heads, and the worst part was that we couldn't tell anyone. We were about to record an album and we didn't want Mercury to question our future and pull the plug. Eventually, thanks to my high school connections in Salt Lake City, we retained the top criminal attorney in the state, who made the charges disappear.

We spent the next year touring constantly, which put my idea of America into sharper focus. America was the land of the free when my band was able to pay a high-end attorney $10,000 to wipe the slate clean on a felony drug charge, or when my band could fly to New York or Los Angeles last minute to play a concert.

But when I sat with my bandmates outside our dirty, smoke-filled Phoenix motel room, watching our next-door neighbors—a pair of methed-out rednecks—show off their guns, America made me fearful for my life.

When I spent two hours at a downtown Memphis jail awaiting the release of my bandmate, who was held on DWI charges, I felt sick to my stomach. Not from the smell of the waiting room or the fact that my good friend had just spent the night behind bars, but because of the people who were released before he was. One by one, young men emerged from the jail's heavy release door. They all walked with the same slow pace and displayed the same face of exhaustion. They all had something else in common too: every one of them was Black. I knew from the week we'd spent recording in Memphis that not all of its Black population was criminal, and that far from all its white population was innocent—on the contrary, I'd been offered drugs, guns, and illegal fireworks exclusively by white people. But for two hours, I waited, expecting to see—eventually *hoping* to see—a white person emerge. I didn't until my friend walked through the door.

ON ONE OF THE LEMONS' early tours, we played at a club in Cambridge called the Middle East. When we arrived, certain elements felt oddly familiar to me: the smell of exotic spices cutting through a fresh cleaning; the way the light sliced through the curtains; the way in which the door opened to Mass. Ave., which also sounded familiar. I called my mother, who confirmed that the Middle East was the same restaurant where we ate frequently during my childhood. The owner, also named Nabil, had become our friend, and my mother and I had been regulars. I'm not sure whether it was my name, the fact that Nabil just liked us, or because we obviously didn't have any money back then. But we never once paid for a meal.

When I asked for Nabil, the bartender looked at me as if something were wrong. Why did I need to talk to the owner? "I'm an old friend," I assured her. I immediately recognized Nabil's wide smile and his black slicked-back hair and I told him my story—that my mother and I used to eat in his restaurant when I was a child. He remembered right away. "You and your mother were always so nice," he said.

To this day, it remains one of the simplest, most nostalgic, reassuring, and complimentary things anyone has said to me. I was comforted and inspired to know that this man—who'd given me and my mother countless free meals—had remained in business for two decades. I imagined and hoped that he'd taken on other cases like ours over the years, passing on his good fortune. That night, my bandmates and I enjoyed a gigantic Middle Eastern feast courtesy of Nabil. There, reunited with the first *other* Nabil I'd ever met, I experienced the true meaning of our shared name: noble, learned, and *generous*.

THE WEEK AFTER MERCURY RELEASED our album in June 1996, the Lemons opened two shows for Joan Jett. Joan was a legend to us—we'd all owned *I Love Rock 'n Roll* when we were kids. Backstage in Santa Cruz, Joan's longtime manager Kenny

Laguna offered nuggets of fatherly rock advice like "A good opening band only plays for twenty minutes" and "Always leave 'em wanting more." Between nuggets, Kenny tried to introduce us to "Joanie." But whenever he called her, she ignored him, oblivious to, or painfully aware of, the four superfans who stood nervously with her manager.

The next night in San Francisco, our friends in the Seattle band 7 Year Bitch were in town and stopped by the venue. They also knew Joan, and when she saw us hanging out with her friends, she let down her guard. That evening I had the surreal honor of seeing tough, tiny, leather-clad Joan Jett standing side stage, shaking her head in time with my kick and snare drum hits.

THE LEMONS NEVER TOOK OFF, but after my three years in the band, I felt like I'd finished a graduate program in the music business. I was the member of the band who spent the most time with our manager. I asked our A&R person questions about how the label functioned and how her job was different from our product manager's. I made our attorney explain the subtleties of our record contract, and how ours differed from other deals. The years I spent in the Lemons were full of invaluable experiences and lessons, and the band served as my next step into the music business.

22.

Sonic Boom Records

I did my job well at Easy Street, but I spent my breaks on the phone doing band business. My coworker Jason Hughes, on the other hand, went above and beyond expectations—he treated the store as if it were his own. Jason had graduated from UC Berkeley with a political economics degree, and he hosted radio shows on two different Seattle stations. He had dark, endearing eyebrows that caused him to look empathetic and honest, and he persevered through painful conversations with customers on the chance that he might turn them on to new albums by Cat Power or Elliott Smith.

One day he frustratingly vented to me that he worked his ass off and our boss Matt didn't seem to notice, and that I did nothing more than I was expected to do and Matt loved me. I agreed, and explained that I loved my job, but that I reserved every moment of personal time to further my own interests. Jason looked at me silently, then he responded with determination: "We should open a record store." That night at a bar, we laid out a simple budget on a napkin, and when we both agreed that we could realistically achieve the small monthly gross income needed to cover our rent, we jumped in.

Neither of us had ever had the fantasy of opening a record store—something most record store owners would claim. But we both wanted to listen to and talk about music all day—and get paid to do so. We managed to scrape up the funds to open the store with credit cards and a loan from Jason's mom, and signed a lease on a tiny retail space on the main floor of a house in Fremont, an artsy, slightly bohemian yuppie community and the only Seattle neighborhood that we thought could sustain a new record store. In September 1997, we opened Sonic Boom Records in Fremont as planned, but just far enough off the beaten path for nobody to notice us. Some days, we played three or four albums—that's how we measured time—without a customer entering the store. Most days, we sat on our couch with nothing to do, inhaling the sweet smell that floated up from our basement, where our landlord Bill baked all of Alaska Airlines' cheesecakes. Bill was known throughout Fremont as, appropriately enough, Cheesecake.

Jason continued to work at Easy Street two days a week, and I worked the front counter at American Music two days a week, ringing up guitar strings for novices and superstars alike. Jason and I shared the same schedule of thirteen days on and one day off. We put everything we could back into the store, sometimes paying ourselves $250 every two weeks—$225 if the store really needed some extra money to expand our Tom Waits section.

For lunch, we often shared one order of cashew chicken from Jai Thai and asked for extra rice. Or Marianne, who managed Rudy's Barbershop next door, would bring us soup from Bagel Oasis across the street. We traded music for meals at the Longshoreman's Daughter, where Jason met his future wife Tes, who waitressed there.

In 1998, Death Cab for Cutie released their debut album *Something about Airplanes*. We proudly and ambitiously ordered ten copies, a huge number for us at the time. Almost immediately, our bet paid off: the band played a packed live in-store and helped establish Sonic Boom as a hub for Northwest indie rock. Nick, the bass player, became one of our first under-the-table employees.

Thanks to our new association with Death Cab, and growing word of mouth about the store, major label A&R people started calling us asking about local bands such as Modest Mouse, Vendetta Red, and Pedro the Lion. We found helping them to be a welcome source of supplemental income and soon had several of their credit cards on file. When we were short on rent money, we loaded up boxes with local music bound for New York and LA. We also held rent parties where we'd trade CDs for a keg from the brewery up the street and invite our friends over for free beer after hours. We were always amazed at how much people spent after a few drinks in a record store.

MTV's *The Real World* shot a season in Seattle for five months in 1998, and one afternoon, the entire cast of early twentysome-things invaded the store, escorted by two Seattle police officers, a camera crew, and an entourage wearing satin jackets and barking into headset microphones. We had a brief, awkward, on-camera discussion about Modest Mouse with "Nathan." But he didn't buy anything and we didn't make the show.

ONE RARE SUNNY AFTERNOON, an obvious out-of-towner entered the store straight off a flight from LAX, donning wrap-around sunglasses and crisp, better-than-Abercrombie gear.

"Hey, listen." He looked both ways and approached us, as if there were other customers in the store. "Limp Bizkit is going to be recording down the street for a while. I'm just doing a walk-around, quietly letting people know what's up. If you see Fred Durst or any of the guys, they just wanna be chill. It's no big deal."

Jason and I nodded slowly. Jason was likely thinking, *I hate that fucking band. He better not come in my store.* And I was thinking, *I hate that fucking band. I hope he comes in my store.*

Word spread around the neighborhood like wildfire. Marianne from Rudy's came tearing into the store, oblivious to the fact that we were now actually busy with a few customers.

"Limp fucking Bizkit!" she screamed, slamming the door with a devilish grin. "Sorry. Hi, everyone."

We never saw Fred, who was dating MTV personality Carmen Electra at the time. Apparently, they got into a very loud, public blowout in Rudy's before Limp Bizkit even started recording its next masterpiece.

"Fuck fucking Seattle!" Mr. Durst commanded, according to the Rudy's crew. "We're fucking out of this shithole!"

THE STORE'S HUMBLE BEGINNINGS of shared lunches and rent parties quickly shifted with the confluence of two events in the early 2000s: we moved to a more central and larger location, and great numbers of Seattleites invested in indie rock as the circle of bands that surrounded the store blew up. Death Cab for Cutie, Sleater-Kinney, Modest Mouse, Elliott Smith, and Built to Spill were our bread and butter, and suddenly we were selling those and other albums by what seemed like the truckload. Many of our bestsellers were albums by Northwest bands; we were in the geographic epicenter of an important musical moment.

Our customer base expanded and included musicians we never imagined we'd interact with on a regular basis. R.E.M.'s guitarist Peter Buck, who now lived in Seattle, once told us he'd walked seven miles to the store to shop—and that his plan for the rest of the day was to walk home and listen to his new records. The recent Seattle transplant Dave Matthews regularly depleted our small world music section. Guns N' Roses' Duff McKagan joined Team Sonic Boom when more than one hundred customers and employees ran a 5K race together, celebrating the store's anniversary. Pearl Jam's bassist Jeff Ament once asked for recommendations, and I gave him two of my current favorite albums: *The Shape of Punk to Come*, the explosive posthumous opus of white noise by Refused; and *Emergency and I*, the artfully tense album by the Dismemberment Plan. A couple of months later, Pearl Jam announced the Dismemberment Plan as the opener on a leg of their world tour.

WHEN THE STORE WAS ON its feet and we needed more money to expand, Jason and I applied for a small-business loan. I wish I could claim Jason's clever idea to tick the opposite boxes on the loan application: Jason, who is white, had been born in South Africa and therefore suggested that he tick the African American box and I tick the White box. "It's a fucked-up question and we won't be lying," he claimed. We didn't get the loan, but we told the story for years.

USED CDs WERE A BIG part of our business, and it was always a welcome surprise when someone sold us a large collection of interesting music. Before pricing the CDs for sale, we'd spend the afternoon better acquainting ourselves with experimentalists like the Residents or artists like Billie Holiday or Shuggie Otis—with whom we were familiar only through greatest hits compilations. When I returned from lunch one afternoon, Jason had bought a sizable collection of jazz CDs, which included a stack by Roy Ayers, with many covers that I'd never seen before. *Virgo Vibes* was released in 1967, *Five years before I was released*, I thought. It featured a strong blue-and-red psychedelic design around my father's head and sounded more like traditional jazz than anything I'd heard of his. The songs had no vocals—instead they featured horns and piano. Every song included a spine-tingling vibes solo.

It was the only album from the stack I listened to that afternoon because I was worried that a customer might ask, "What's this playing right now?" That question is the highest compliment any record store clerk can hope for. But when the album is by your nonexistent father whom you'd rather not talk about, you keep it in the stack.

I listened to several more of Roy's albums in my car and at home over the next few days, but when I was done, I priced each one for sale. Listening to my father's music made me feel closer to him. But the exercise felt complete. I didn't want to listen to his albums enough to either grow to love them or become tired of them. I just needed to hear them once.

SEATTLE WAS A VERY WHITE CITY, and I sometimes wondered how people viewed me as a non-white business owner. The same way I feared the reactions of my high school dates' parents when I arrived at their door, I also feared a situation in which my race might place me at a disadvantage. Solicitors always looked shocked to meet me when they asked to see the owner, but Jason got the same reaction—we were both young and wore band T-shirts.

When a white, middle-aged male label representative asked me, "Hey, Nabil, where are all the Black women in Seattle?" I let it roll over me. He asked so innocently and honestly. As if I were simply expected to know—as if they actually existed and I knew their secret location. Rather than getting angry about his perception of who I was, I told him honestly that he needed to move to a different city. I had lived in mostly white neighborhoods in Seattle, but I was always surprised when I attended large public events and didn't see more non-white people. Seattle Supersonics basketball games and Seattle Mariners baseball games felt far more white than the New York Yankees games I'd attended with my uncle as a child. The many concerts I saw were attended by predominately white audiences—even when the performers weren't white.

The buttoned-up Seattle mayor who was up for reelection once entered the store with an entourage that included a photographer. After a brief conversation in which the white mayor made earnest, concerned faces while asking what challenges we faced as a Seattle business, a pushy assistant placed me—not Jason—at his side for a series of photos. The mayor's office soon called, asking permission to use our photo in his campaign flyer, which I assumed was going to the white, liberal neighborhoods surrounding our store. We joked that his campaign slogan would read "Some of my best friends are half-Black."

Late one night, I received a call from our alarm company telling me that someone had broken into the store. I arrived to find our door smashed in and our cash register in pieces on the hard tile floor. The voice inside my head dictated a different protocol than Jason's would have: *Wait outside, identify yourself, and greet the police when they arrive.* Even in safe, liberal Seattle, I didn't want to be the non-white person caught crouching over the pieces of a cash register when the police arrived. That's how you get shot.

One day, a white Sonic Boom employee got into an altercation with a non-white customer. The noise caused me to run down from the office. The customer claimed he'd received a discount at the store before, but that it wasn't offered today, and the clerk was therefore racist. I knew that our discount policy was fairly indiscriminate and therefore wildly inconsistent. I also knew that our employee wasn't racist. I asked the customer to step outside.

In that moment, I thought back to Alan's behavior in his confrontation over Smiths concert tickets with Bleecker Bob—the man he'd verbally disarmed by taking things down a notch, rather than turning them up. I deliberately spoke slower and lowered the volume of my voice. "Look at me," I said, pointing to my face. "I own this store. You think this shit doesn't happen to me too?"

He stared at me for a moment—and during those long few seconds, I knew we were each trying to determine the race of the man who stood before us. Then he slowly nodded his head, accepting my identity as similar enough to his—and he apologized for over-reacting. He also apologized to the clerk and we gave him his discount. He promised he'd be back soon, citing that we had the best hip-hop selection in town. Our clerk was still shaken up, but I was more concerned with myself. "I don't know what I just told him," I confessed to her. "That shit has *never* happened to me."

I felt guilty about the reasoning I'd used, and even though experiencing microaggressions was common, I felt I didn't have a compelling, true story to tell about experiencing overt racism.

SONIC BOOM EXPANDED QUICKLY—maybe too quickly. By 2003 we had three locations and twenty-three employees. One of them had a stalker who hid creepy, crayon-drawn notes to him in our CD bins. Another had to be fired on his birthday. Two of them needed to be pulled apart before a fistfight broke out on the store floor. One of them may have saved another one's life during a seizure. Two staff couples got married (and divorced).

Sonic Boom had developed such an industry presence that not only did Hollywood Records send us regular free shipments of the Polyphonic Spree's excellent debut album, new customers whom we perceived as fake started coming in to buy them from us. We had to email the label:

> Dear, Hollywood Records:
>
> Thank you for the free Polyphonic Spree CD's. Please keep them coming. You might be surprised to hear that people actually like this album, so please stop sending in fake customers who are depleting our stock.
>
> Kind regards. Sonic Boom Records.

AT THAT TIME, it was commonplace for bands to play free live in-stores, and though they were always stressful due to noise complaints, overcrowding, and the fact that people rarely bought anything at the events, these remain some of my fondest record store memories. We never quite got used to the fact that if we asked nicely enough, Joanna Newsom would drag her harp onto our modest stage, early in her career, and perform. Or that the well-established British band Supergrass would play its only American in-store of their tour at Sonic Boom.

Saul Williams gave an intense, inspiring performance the night George W. Bush was reelected. Punk icon Nikki Sudden refused to put out his cigarette when he entered the store, insisting, "Without cigarettes, there would be no rock and roll!" An elderly woman fainted during classical violinist Hilary Hahn's packed-beyond-capacity performance, returning the next day with her lawyer son . . . to apologize.

Sonic Boom started to appear on high-profile Best Record Store lists in *Rolling Stone*, *SPIN*, and *The Wall Street Journal*. Our business was booming, and Jason and I were making money. We were both out of debt before thirty and did the best we could to take care of our employees by offering health insurance and a 401(k) retirement plan. We also threw a lot of parties.

It felt crazy—and scary—to stop and think that what started as a conversation one day between two twenty-five-year-olds at our eight-dollars-per-hour record store jobs had led to this: in just a few years, we'd built a small empire. In addition to our employees, we had a bookkeeper, an accountant, an attorney, three different landlords, and hundreds of vendors to deal with. It was a lot more responsibility than we'd planned on, and the reality was that we were somehow largely responsible for the livelihood of dozens of people and that income came from trans-actions averaging just thirty dollars each. Though I didn't al-ways think it was fair to Jason, my first priority was still to play in a band, and the store allowed me that flexibility. Sometimes when I went on tour, the store suffered from my monthlong ab-sence. But to Jason's and our staff's credit, the store was in ca-pable hands when I was gone.

23.

Smooth Criminal

The Lemons had toured with San Francisco punk-pop band the Meices and I'd become a big fan watching them from the side of the stage every night. When Joe, the singer, started his new band, Alien Crime Syndicate (ACS), his new songs were undeniably big rock songs with distorted guitars, but with structure and melody. When the drummer left and Joe moved to Seattle, I naturally jumped onto the drum seat.

Joe's shoulder-length sandy-blond hair and pastel pants and shirts could have just as easily placed him on a surfboard as on a stage. Jeff, the bassist—who wore all black and had dyed black hair—was more rock and roll than I was, but then most people were. ACS was another band in which my hair separated me visually, but I got along great with the guys and loved playing with them.

ACS grew quickly in Seattle and down the West Coast. Rather than feeling stuck when no label wanted to sign us, we self-released an album and toured a ton, booking our own shows across the country. The touring was rough—four of us and all our equipment packed into a van. We stuffed into one cheap motel room, slept on our friends' floors, or stayed with the often creepy late-night people we met at the show. I was financially stable—due to Sonic Boom's recent success—but typically I did what my bandmates did. We were touring together, and that meant living off of what we made.

When Death Cab for Cutie's drummer left, Nick the bass player asked me if I was interested in trying out. I loved Death Cab, who were on the rise. But so was ACS, to whom I'd committed and spent time building. I sometimes wonder how different my life would be if I'd auditioned and been asked to join Death Cab, who are still hugely successful in their third decade.

BY LATE 2001, Joe had written a new batch of songs, and we decided again that rather than wait around for label interest, we should make a new album and jump back into touring. This time, though, I decided I'd start my own label. I owned a record store, which allowed me to watch more closely how music was manufactured, marketed, and distributed. I knew music journalists and radio programmers in town. And I could afford to get it off the ground.

I hired a publicist and a radio promoter, pressed two thousand CDs, and released the album myself on a label I named the Control Group. Almost immediately, the Seattle commercial radio station KNDD started to play our single as did other alternative stations down the West Coast, including the influential Los Angeles station KROQ. Then major labels started to court ACS. Just one month after I released our album, ACS signed to the much larger label V2, then home of the White Stripes and Moby. V2 then bought the rights to my ACS album from me for $100,000. Suddenly, I was again playing drums in a band signed to a major label.

Though $100,000 did seem like a ton of money, I'd already owned a business for five years and knew that it wasn't as much as it sounded like. Our band business manager told me to set aside one third of it for taxes. With the remainder, I decided to buy all the drum gear I wanted. Still, that didn't make a significant dent, so I set the rest aside to release records by other bands.

Our album was released by V2 on May 21, 2002. ACS shot a music video for the single "Ozzy" that cost more than most houses at the time. We heard our own song on the radio and on the hit MTV reality show *The Osbournes*. And we spent most of the next year on the road, always in search of a better tour. We were never offered a tour opening for Foo Fighters or a similar big alt-rock band, which everyone agreed would be perfect, but we stayed busy.

Our first tour after the album was released was opening for Sugar Ray at Six Flags amusement parks and midwestern state colleges. Sugar Ray was a Southern California party band who became huge playing sunny, laid-back frat party anthems. They'd had several hit songs—each sung by their handsome, surf-model-like singer Mark McGrath—and though we knew they weren't a *cool* band, we loved the idea of playing large venues to mainstream audiences. We all laughed when our sound guy asked what songs Sugar Ray sang and the answers flew out of our mouths like guilty pleasures: to this day, "Fly," "Every Morning," and "Someday" remain stuck in my head.

The first show was at Bemidji State University in a rural Minnesota town one hundred miles south of the Canadian border. Backstage in a hockey locker room, we sat, bored, picking at a deli tray, waiting to sound check and wondering what these shows would be like without alcohol—the university had made its no-alcohol-on-campus policy quite clear upon our arrival. A loud noise interrupted the silence in our brightly lit room and the presence of an overly confident human turned our heads.

"What's up, guys! I'm Mark." There he was: Sugar Ray leader Mark McGrath looking *exactly* like he looked on MTV. He slammed a case of beer down loudly on a locker room bench as if to say, *Look, it's me!* His huge smile was eclipsed only by his firm handshake, and as much as I wanted to make fun of him, he had it—that presence. I *wanted* to like Mark McGrath. And why shouldn't I? Suddenly I felt a little bad inside for making fun of Sugar Ray with my friends. Mark was incredibly welcoming— much more so than most headlining bands on tours I've been on.

We talked for a while and I recounted a story. "I saw Sugar Ray on your first time through Seattle in 1995, I think. You played this *tiny* club called the Rendezvous." As I told him, I remembered the show well. It was in the afternoon and the room was packed with people that the record company had begged to come have free drinks and appetizers and see their new signing, Sugar Ray. At Easy Street, it was my job to attend such functions, and when I arrived late, Mark called me out and shouted something clever like "This guy came in late and he has the smallest penis!"

"That was a fun show," said Mark, still smiling. "Wasn't the club called the Jewelbox, though?" Technically, he was right, the Jewelbox was the theater inside the Rendezvous. It's no surprise that Mark went on to an impressive winning streak on *Rock & Roll Jeopardy!*

AFTER SEVERAL SHOWS, we couldn't decide which was more fun, the colleges or the amusement parks.

The colleges were "Spring Flings": year-end free concerts for students, typically held in large arenas. Thousands of students showed up every night, and we quickly learned that drunk midwestern college kids made great audiences—there were no music snobs at the Sugar Ray shows. After the shows we sold dozens of CDs and signed autographs. Then we went out to bars on the strip—every small town had one—where we enjoyed our celebrity status when people recognized us from earlier in the night.

Alternately, at the amusement parks we could skip the line at any attraction. After sound check, the four of us would zip through three or four rides in under thirty minutes, escorted from ride to ride via secretive backroads on a golf cart. When we arrived at an attraction, we'd be placed immediately at the front: four men in our thirties cutting off hordes of patiently waiting kids.

The amusement park audiences were drastically different from the college audiences: they were mostly kids and their parents. The crowds were equally large—a few thousand people— and we realized that we were the first live band that many of these kids had ever seen. At some of the amusement park shows, we sold more than one hundred CDs and had a line of people waiting. It was low-hanging fruit at all of the shows—children who'd never seen a band and drunk college kids. But it still felt good to make a connection with people. We knew we weren't a cool indie band, but our goal had been exactly the opposite: we wanted to reach *everyone*. The Sugar Ray tour was a good start. That being said, it was also somewhat depressing—it wasn't a *real* tour.

ACS played weird, short runs of shows in order to remain active: a few in empty Midwest clubs supporting the washed-up eighties Hollywood glam rockers Faster Pussycat. At a show in Flint, Michigan, we supported the costumed metal band Mushroomhead, who played spastic, angry, ostensibly scary metal but who turned out to be extremely nice people. There was a one-off at the two-hundred-capacity San Diego club the Casbah opening for Weezer on a warm-up reunion show before *The Green Album* came out. I'd always been a big fan and felt especially lucky that night when I got to watch the band's sound check—which was nearly as long as their entire set—with just a few other people in the room.

. . .

AFTER TOURING WITH SUGAR RAY, we were scheduled to do a monthlong tour with three other "up-and-coming alternative bands." When the bands are all around the same level, it's called a package tour; in this case, the package was quite light. The tour was like a reality show on which bands were eliminated, except on our tour, they did so by choice. We started on the West Coast, and band number one literally did not show up. After just two poorly attended shows, band number two disappeared, aware that the next month of their lives would be spent driving around a huge country playing for nobody. Band number three dropped off after Denver, when the singer was sucker punched by a skinhead outside the club.

That left us with two weeks of shows to play on our own. In Chicago, we were booked at the House of Blues, a large venue that we knew we had no chance of filling with the full four-band bill, let alone by ourselves. We loaded in, sound checked, and returned to our hotel, which was connected to the venue. An hour later, our tour manager called to say the show was canceled. "They're paying us our guarantee. They just don't want to open the club because it's expensive to pay their staff when they know it won't be crowded." Our backstage room at the venue was already full of deli trays, chips, beer, and all of the familiar items that we'd planned to eat for dinner that night. Someone jokingly shouted, "Have them send the rider up to our hotel room!" Five minutes later, two people arrived with everything from our backstage room.

A hotel room that smelled like a backstage room somehow made the night even more depressing.

There's a brilliant moment in the film *This Is Spinal Tap* when the on-the-decline British band is on tour in the American Midwest. Their concerts aren't selling well, some are canceled, and morale is low. When one of their older songs comes on the radio, the band feels newly elevated, important, content. They feel justified in their years of hard work. The band gleefully quiets down to listen to the DJ's comments after the song, and they're quickly pulled back into reality when the DJ says about the band, who have just released a new album, "Currently residing in the 'where are they now' file . . ."

That's how I felt in Chicago. I'd spent my entire life wanting to play drums in a *real* band and I'd now done it twice. Both times, I'd signed to a major record label—something most people don't even come close to doing once. I knew how fortunate I was to also own a record store and a newly funded record label, but those were my second and third ambitions. Playing drums had always been number one. But as I sat in that crowded Chicago hotel room, a plate of wilting cheese in front of me, I felt heavily dejected.

The next morning we started the long drive back to Seattle. Little in my life has felt more fruitless than driving across America in a hot van with three friends, knowing that we'd all just exhausted our last opportunity. That the label would soon pull the plug. That we had worked our asses off and had a shot, but we were on our own again, thousands of miles from home. It happened with the Lemons and it happened again with ACS.

The only upside was that when it finally happened, our label paid us handsomely to break their contract with us.

IN 2004, THOUGH WE no longer had the backing of a major label, ACS released a new album and scored a coveted slot opening one of the first US shows on Pixies' reunion tour. Backstage in Spokane, Washington, I heard Kim Deal's powerful, distinctive voice from Pixies' nearby dressing room. But I was too nervous to walk in and say hello. Kim's voice—the same one I'd heard for the first time as a teenager in my friend's mom's Volvo—stood out to me, ringing like a sharp bell but with warmth and empathy. Kim Deal in real life sounded exactly like Kim Deal on her albums, and I was in awe from the room next door to hers.

WHEN ACS TOURED the West Coast that spring, the former Replacements bassist Tommy Stinson was backstage at our LA show. Tommy—who had cofounded the Replacements when he was thirteen, and was currently the longtime bassist in the *new* Guns N' Roses—had just finished his first solo album. He wanted to tour but didn't want to go through the financial and logistical hassle of hiring a backing band. "What if you guys were my backing band and you also opened the shows?" Tommy suggested.

A few months later, ACS embarked on a five-week tour opening for and also backing Tommy Stinson. But before we played a show, we flew to LA to play Tommy's single "Motivation" on

The Late Late Show with Craig Kilborn. I'd never played on network TV—none of us had. I'd been told how awkward and difficult it could be to play one song in a sterile, brightly lit, air-conditioned studio in front of a seated audience that's not there to see you. But we were prepared—we rehearsed tirelessly with Tommy, and I rented a beautiful silver-sparkle vintage Gretsch drum kit. I jumped up and down repeatedly backstage to warm up just before walking onto the brisk stage. I wasn't nervous. I knew we'd kill it, and those four minutes stand out as some of the most exhilarating in my life.

We honed the set for the American tour over the course of a couple of weeks. It was a blast. Sometimes we took no break between sets, and ACS would play for forty-five minutes straight into an hourlong Tommy Stinson set. I was in the best drumming shape I'd ever been in, playing to packed clubs almost every night.

However, every night, I'd face an unsettling moment as fans shouted out the names of Replacements songs that I didn't know. The Minneapolis band was legendary during my teenage years and I should have paid attention, but they'd somehow passed me by. Tommy insisted that he'd never play a Replacements song, but every night, I worried that the increasingly pushy audience would win and Tommy would turn around and say, "Fuck it, let's play 'Alex Chilton.' One, two, three, four! . . ."

After a sold-out New York City show, we boarded a flight to London, where I'd only been once as a tourist. When we woke up at the infamous rock star haunt the Columbia hotel, a gigantic all-white double-decker tour bus awaited us outside. Nobody in my band had toured in a bus before—we had our years of experience driving all night only in overcrowded, garbage-filled band vans. Even though it wasn't ours alone, the bus was a significant milestone. I made toast when I wanted to. We didn't need to pull over to pee. If I didn't like the movie playing in the downstairs lounge, I'd see what people were watching in the upstairs lounge. The irony was that in the UK, the drives were so short. I would have loved to have had that bus in America, where we routinely drove six to eight hours between shows every day.

ACS ended on a high note. We never broke up and nobody quit—we just all started doing other things. I remain friends with the members, all of whom still play music. Like I had in the Lemons, I paid a lot of attention to the business side of ACS, and I was more deeply embedded because I'd released our album myself before selling it to V2.

WHEN ACS WENT DORMANT in 2005, I immediately went on the hunt for a new band. I never stopped to think that I was now thirty-three, arguably over the hill for many rock bands, or that with my business partner, Jason, I ran a successful record store, which took a serious amount of time and energy, or that I had my own record label with enough funding to take risks on some new bands. I'd now been in two *real* bands that had allowed me to play drums for a living, make records, and tour, which is more than most musicians get to do. But neither band had achieved what I considered true success. Neither had achieved ubiquity.

Why did I need to join another band? Where did my ambition

and drive come from—my *need* to work? Alan was a talented and disciplined musician, but he didn't have this kind of drive.

It had to be from Roy.

Roy was now sixty-five years old, and I knew he still toured the world. When I was a child and met Roy, he never sat me down and explained to me his motivation. But I felt it, and I recognized our similarities. I needed to join a new band because I needed to play. I needed to keep things moving forward. It was literally in my blood.

24.

Putting the Days to Bed

In 2005 I joined an established Seattle band called the Long Winters. I'd become friendly with John, the larger-than-life singer, guitarist, and songwriter whom *Magnet* magazine once called "Bob Dylan in a hoodie." John wrote strong melodies and clever lyrics that came together as muscular songs that still fell under the indie rock umbrella.

The Long Winters had already released two albums on Barsuk Records—the Seattle label that was enjoying an impressive run with albums by Death Cab for Cutie and Nada Surf—and they'd toured extensively in North America and Europe. After I completed one American tour with the band, we went into the studio to record the 2006 album *Putting the Days to Bed*.

Once the album was released, we spent two weeks supporting

the British keyboard-driven pop band Keane in the arenas of Europe, where our van looked like a toy parked beside Keane's three tour buses and several semitrucks. Backstage at the first show in Paris, we learned that their three-piece band traveled with a twenty-person crew, three of whom were full-time chefs. The band also had a burly security guard who never smiled and who followed them everywhere. Every night the stage was carefully lined with glow-in-the-dark tape that we were told *never* to cross for fear that we might stumble into Keane's delicate and expensive lighting gear.

The members of Keane were kind and generous, thanking us from the stage every night during their set and giving us each a brand new iPod on the last night of the tour—well, their assistant actually handed us the iPods. To us, Keane was on top of the world. But when they returned to the tour from a quick trip to open for U2, everyone's perspective shifted. Keane described U2's crew and production in great, awestruck detail, and it apparently dwarfed their own. Every band has their sights on someone else; there's always someone bigger, and music is a competitive game. The Long Winters envied some of our peers, and surely there were smaller bands who'd have loved to be as big as we were.

On the nights between Keane shows, we headlined smaller clubs. We'd play a tight forty-minute opening set at a ten-thousand-capacity arena in Rotterdam one night, then headline a three-hundred-capacity smoke-filled club in Groningen the next. Because the Keane shows were so regimented, we took more liberties at the headline shows, sometimes playing for more than two hours. Between songs John charmed audiences with local phrases and in-side jokes he'd somehow picked up. In Vienna we played a very long, impromptu version of "Stairway to Heaven." "What's it going to take to get you guys to leave?" John asked the audience, which only made them applaud more.

Those shows were the most comfortable I've ever felt playing drums. After one hundred or so shows, there's a sense of safety that kicks in—a self-assurance that no matter what one band member does, the others will react accordingly and it will come together. Or at least it will fall apart in an entertaining way.

RACE DYNAMICS WERE LESS on my mind in Europe, where even gas stations and small towns felt safe. But in America, things hadn't changed much since my tours with my previous bands. The Long Winters played legendary venues like the Greek Theatre in Los Angeles and the Ryman Auditorium in Nashville, where, from the stage, bright light shot into the large theater through church-like stained glass windows. On the front of the balcony, a sign read in all caps: 1897 CONFEDERATE GALLERY. It faced the stage, reminding every performer of Tennessee's seem-ingly proud Confederate history. It gave me an uncomfortable chill. I tried to ignore my bad feelings during our set, but I couldn't. The sign—which was removed in 2007—was a glaring reminder to anyone who set foot on that stage of slavery and of America's unfortunate ability to uplift and glorify shameful rem-nants from its past.

Van drives across the country with the Long Winters felt the same as the ones I'd known: big cities were great, every other place was suspect. Once, somewhere in Nebraska, I woke up early and went to breakfast by myself at the diner next to our motel. There's not much alone time on tour, and I enjoyed my thirty minutes of solitude, while my middle-aged, round-faced waitress brought me eggs, toast, and coffee. I left eleven dollars cash under the saltshaker—more than enough to cover the $8.69 check—and I wandered back to the hotel, where my bandmates were now awake and hungry. I recommended the place next door—there was no other option. When I joined them later at their large table, I noticed our waitress and a man who appeared to be the manager standing in the kitchen entrance and staring at us. The manager had dyed blond hair and a spray tan, and they spoke swiftly, with furrowed brows. When the waitress walked over, my heart rate began to increase—I'm not sure why; I knew I hadn't done anything wrong.

The waitress spoke firmly to me. "Did you wanna take care of that check?"

"I left eleven dollars on the table!" My voice raised in defense. I patted my pockets, which felt like the right thing to do when accused of something to do with money. "I left you a twenty-five percent tip!" The manager stood in the kitchen entrance, watching. Then the waitress walked away. I explained to my bandmates that I'd left eleven dollars on the table and they all nodded, but I could feel our collective tension. No matter how petty or false the accusation was, who would the small-town sheriff believe?

"Do you think I skipped out on my tab and then *came back*

half an hour later?" I asked our waitress as she approached us again, now holding a full pot of coffee.

"I'm so sorry." Her hand shook as she filled our cups. Her voice was lower and more quiet than before. "There's been a misunderstanding. Your coffee and anything else you want is on me." Then she quickly disappeared.

"I guess she found the eleven dollars?" I said naively to the table.

"She never lost your eleven dollars." John said after he sipped his coffee. "She saw you—the dark guy with the funny glasses— as the perfect mark, and she told her manager that you skipped out on your check. The eleven dollars was in her pocket the whole time." The rest of our faces lit up as John explained the crime he'd just solved. I felt my face droop from a happy *everything is OK* to a depressing *I was just targeted as a scammer and a thief because of how I look*. That truth sunk in, and my prevailing thought was highly pragmatic: *Because of how I look, I can never leave cash on the table for a server again.*

IN MANY WAYS, the Long Winters was the happiest I'd ever been playing in a band. We were just some Seattle indie guys and I fit right in—I wasn't even the only member who wore glasses. The Lemons and ACS were both shooting for the stars—signing to major record labels and fully immersing ourselves in the game. When the goal is for your music to be on commercial radio stations and MTV, you do things differently and allow more people to inform your decisions. The Lemons and ACS needed the machine to work for us.

The Long Winters were ambitious, and we were surrounded by great people who worked hard, but the band didn't rely as much on external forces. There was a tremendous satisfaction in the lack of bluffing that went on in the Long Winters. We were a real band with real fans.

25.

Love Will Bring Us Back Together

Every year or two, I noticed Roy Ayers in the listings for the Seattle venue Jazz Alley. I'd never considered going to one of my father's concerts—not even as an anonymous, ticket-buying fan. I never thought about seeing who he was and what he'd become, or checking if I could still feel his magnetism from the back row. He was nobody to me—as generic as the other artists listed who I'd heard of but with whom I had no connection.

Someone once told me a story about my father in Seattle: Roy had played multiple nights at Jazz Alley, and on the final night, he hadn't yet been paid for any of the shows. He walked onstage to greet the sold-out crowd, and then demanded—in front of everyone—that the owner walk onstage and pay him, and that the performance wouldn't begin until this happened. A mix of applause for my father and jeers at the club owner filled the room until a man in a suit nervously rushed onstage and handed over a fat envelope full of cash.

It's a story I retold every time people asked me if I was going to see my father play, as if I were sharing a legend about Elvis or James Brown. Telling it was a way to change the subject—to avoid my real feelings in favor of a story about a musical legend that led to an impressed chuckle, removing me from any potential discomfort.

WHEN I WAS THIRTY-FOUR, I started seeing a therapist for the first time. My therapist, of course, wanted me to open up about my father, sensing an obvious gap in which to root around. In those sessions I tried to be open, claiming the same arguments I always have: *I've known my mother and father's arrangement for my entire life. He never left us. My uncle is my father figure. How can someone who's never been there be missing?*

Not long into these therapy sessions, a Sonic Boom employee brought up my father. I remember exactly where I was standing—at the front counter of the store—and where she was standing—above the C section, stapling up a poster.

"I saw that your father's coming to the Triple Door," she said casually, punctuated by a staple gun slamming a staple into the wall.

I was immediately shaken by the nonchalant way in which she mentioned my father. *Doesn't she know my story?* I wondered, as I decided how to respond. I'd always brushed off the idea of my father when someone brought him up, making sure they knew he wasn't a big deal to me. *Yeah, he's my father. Nah, we don't know each other. Nothing bad happened, that was just the arrangement with my mom.* But that day, for some reason, it hit hard.

"Oh, really?" I tried to appear occupied, unfazed, cavalier. Usually when I heard this news, I'd never felt an urge to find out where or when my father was playing. I'd never checked the date to see if I'd be in town or not. He'd pass through and I'd hear about him coming again in another year or two.

But this time, for the first time, I felt a pull. It was a new, unfamiliar feeling—as if someone had told me, "There's a set of beautiful, vintage drums sitting outside with a FREE sign on them. But you can only have them if you act really cool. Don't let on to anyone how badly you want them. Oh, and each drum is stuffed with hundred-dollar bills."

"When is he playing?" I asked calmly.

"September 6."

My mind raced as I pretended to read some papers. "I have to run upstairs for a minute, can you watch the floor?" I walked at a normal pace, trying desperately not to show my rush for the money-stuffed drums, diligently walking up the stairs to the office. There, I quickly confirmed that on September 6, 2006, I'd be in town.

The easy path would have been to ignore it, as I had for so many years. There was no risk in *not* seeing my father. I could make plans to travel to Portland, LA, or New York on that date and tell anyone who asked that I'd be out of town. But now, this new pull existed. For the first time in my life, I wanted to contact my father.

I was now in my midthirties, which meant he was nearing seventy. When I heard about his concert, I didn't think, *He'll be back in a year or two*, like I always had. Instead I thought, *He could be dead before there's a next time*. I imagined what that would feel like. I'd recently been to a checkup, at which my doctor asked about my father's medical history. I answered the same way I had my whole life: "I don't know anything about my father's medical history." But if my father died, I would never find out that information. In fact, I probably wouldn't get a call from anyone. I'd likely find out from a customer—one of the many self-employed musicians or designers who ritualistically read internet news in the morning and then came by the shop around 11:00 a.m. to talk about music while sipping their coffee. "Man, I'm sorry to hear about your dad," they'd say. And I'd likely play along, rather than further expose our lack of connection. I imagined my face becoming hot and my stomach twisting as I walked to the computer to search my father's name, followed by the word "death."

This might be my only chance to ever sit with him, face to face, as an adult. I used that pragmatic line of thinking as an excuse—a way to force myself to finally reach out to my father and ask him the questions I've never been able to ask about him, about myself, about both of our disconnected lives.

I didn't know what I wanted from him. I knew he'd never be my father. It was too late for that, and I'd already grown up around excellent male role models. I didn't need or want money from him. But it felt okay to not have a specific goal in mind. My mother always encouraged me to network—to go on informational interviews and meet with people, even if I wasn't after something specific. So, with my therapist's encouragement and no goal in mind, I set out to schedule an informational interview with my own father, whom I hadn't seen in over two decades, since I was eleven years old.

MY MOTHER WAS the first person I spoke to about the potential meeting. Unlike me, she kept tabs on my father. She didn't stay in touch, but I knew that she'd seen Roy at least once recently when he performed in Berkeley. She showed up with my band's most recent CD to say hello and update him on how her son was doing, and she reported back that he was friendly but brief, as he had been each of the several times I'd met him.

My mother's tone surprised me. She didn't know how to reach my father and became quite protective, warning me about the quest on which I was about to embark. "Be careful! Even if you do get a hold of him, he's so unreliable. Even if you make plans with him . . . he won't come. Are you sure you want to do this?"

My mother had always been a worrier, but she'd never vocally worried about any interest I might have had in Roy. Maybe that was because I'd expressed virtually no interest until now. That day, I could tell just how afraid she was of seeing her son hurt or disappointed.

The only contact I could find online was for my father's booking agent. I didn't want to overwhelm him by saying, "He's my father," and I also thought that I might not be the first person in his life to send such an email. So I typed what I felt was a very simple email that my father would understand if he saw it:

> Hi. This is Nabil. My mother Louise knows Roy from the
> Seventies in New York City. I live in Seattle and I see that Roy is
> coming to play here in September. I'd like to meet up with him at
> some point. Could you please put him in touch with me?
> Thank you.

The moment I pressed send, thirty-four years of not caring about my father came to a close. For the first time, I'd put myself out there. I felt a physical wave of urgency. My throat and chest went dark, my mouth dry. I'd opened a door, and now it was no longer up to me. It was up to my father.

I immediately emailed a friend who worked at the Triple Door, the venue where my father was scheduled to play. I quickly poured out my story and my concern that I might not get a reply. And if that was the case, I asked that I have a backstage pass so I could follow through, without relying on my father.

He obliged and I breathed a big sigh, allowing the chest-throat feelings to dissipate a bit. I had to maintain some level of control over the situation and not leave it all in the hands of the man my mother insisted was self-centered and unreliable. I dreaded the night that was still a month away, on which I might have to crash my own father's concert.

For the next two days I thought about it constantly. I was distracted at work. It was the only topic I discussed with my close friends. After not receiving a reply in two days, I knew I couldn't sit still for another twenty-eight. I went from writing a cool and collected email to one that sounded far more desperate—even threatening. This time I divulged that Roy was my father and that I was coming to the show whether I heard from him or not. And that we'd both be a lot more comfortable at the show if I *did* hear from him.

Fifteen minutes later I received a reply from the agent saying he'd forwarded my email to my father.

I was elated. I asked my mother to please stop asking me if I'd heard back from him—her nervousness was too much on top of my own. And I convinced myself that there was nothing more I could do until the day of the show. I needed, for my own mental health, to completely put it out of my mind.

A week before the show, I woke up to a missed call and a voicemail.

"Hey, Nabil." His voice lifted when he said my name and I was happy that he pronounced it correctly. "This is Roy calling from New York. I heard you're in Seattle." His tone was conversational, as if he were actually speaking to me, not a machine. "I'm gonna be there next week, so give me a call and we can get together. All right, I'll talk to you soon. Bye."

I played Roy's message a few more times to see if I could hear my voice in his. It was such a surprise to hear from him, and so bizarre to actually listen to the voice of the person who helped make me—not on one of his albums, but on my phone, actually speaking to me. He spoke with the warmth and relaxed pace of a man in his sixties.

I smiled through my workout that morning. My five-minute walk to the store felt bouncier than it had in weeks. I arrived, spent thirty minutes on morning emails, made a few quick phone calls, looked at the closing paperwork from the day before, and did everything I could to clear my head before calling my father back.

My stomach was full of nervous energy as the phone rang.

He picked up quickly. "Hello?" It was the same voice that I'd listened to a few times that morning.

Our conversation flowed. It was easy, natural, even fun. At the same time, it felt unreal, like talking to Santa Claus: I wasn't positive that the person I was talking to actually existed. He asked me about living in Seattle and playing music, and I was surprised that he remembered anything about me. He sounded genuinely interested.

There was so much that I wanted to know about his life: His other kids. His health. His history and relationship with music. But I don't remember what I asked him, only that our call was short and it ended with a plan for me to pick him up at his hotel for lunch on the day of the show.

Then I called my mother, who demonstrated even more concern than earlier, before she asked the scariest question: "What are you going to do if he doesn't show up?"

WHEN THE DAY CAME and I made the final turn toward my father's hotel, I became fully aware of my lack of nervousness. I didn't feel short of breath. My stomach felt normal—I was even a little hungry. I lifted my right hand off the steering wheel and held it directly in front of my eyes to see if it was shaking: nope, solid as a rock.

In the wide, covered drop-off loop of Roy's hotel, parents dragged children and luggage through automatic sliding glass doors. Business travelers balanced iced Starbucks drinks and briefcases while talking on their phones. I parked behind a van that was unloading a pack of tourists who wore matching white outfits.

I took a final deep breath, like I would have before a job interview or before walking onstage. But I could tell during the exhale that I didn't need it. When I entered the lobby, I immediately made eye contact with someone who smiled my smile at me. There was no question that the man was Roy. My father. I returned his smile and walked toward him.

"Hi, Roy."

"Nabil, how you doing?" His voice was welcoming.

I laughed a friendly chuckle and shook my head. I didn't know how else to react to holding the hand of the person who helped create me. A hand I didn't think I'd ever touched. We didn't look exactly alike, but I quickly registered the obvious similarities: our high cheekbones, our full brown eyes, and our big, easy smiles. I thought, *Is this what I'm going to look like in thirty years?* His handshake carried a lot of strength and energy.

"You want to get a photo?" Roy noticed the camera that I'd forgotten I held in my hand. I'd hoped to get a picture with him, but I wasn't sure why I'd brought it into the hotel with me. I handed the camera off to a tourist, who snapped two quick shots of men who both loved to have their picture taken.

In the photo, Roy is husky and solid, a bit shorter than me, with a full face that reminded me of what I looked like without glasses. In fact, I thought, *He looks like he should be wearing glasses.* He's standing still, but his constant, animated motion is obvious: his mouth is slightly open as if he'd just caused everyone in the room to burst with laughter. His right hand clutches a cell phone near his chest and gives a thumbs-up sign. Our matching bright smiles and our interchangeable eyes don't compensate for our similarly receding hairlines. He's lost his signature seventies sideburns, but I still have mine. His light mustache and bejeweled silver necklace work together like a matching set.

My favorite sushi restaurant was closed, so we drove to another one nearby, which wasn't as good, and I worried that my father would be less impressed, since he'd originally suggested sushi.

Seated across from each other, we quickly covered the basics: Roy was sixty-six. I was thirty-four. My mother was fifty-five. My uncle Alan was fifty-three. I'd gone to college. I'd played drums all my life, and I currently played in a band called the Long Winters. I co-owned a small chain of record stores and ran my own small record label.

Roy read the credits on the Long Winters CD I'd just handed him. "Oh yeah," he said casually. "Louise told me you changed your name to Ayers." It hadn't occurred to me that my name change might come up. I'd changed my last name so long ago. Nobody ever asked about it.

"Yeah, Braufman was a pain-in-the-ass name so I changed it when I graduated from high school. I wanted to pick another

name I had a connection to." I said this quite tentatively, awaiting Roy's response.

"That's cool." His eyebrows raised as he continued to exam-
ine the CD.

"You got this a lot younger than I did." Roy pointed to his
mostly bald head with mocking emphasis and we both smiled
wide. The smiles—there had already been many—were electrifying moments for me. Moments when I could completely see
pieces of myself in this person who had been so distant for so
long but always somehow present.

Then I began my important but casual interview. There were
things I wanted to know: his background, family life, and music
career. And there were things I *needed* to know: his health history.

He had no problem opening up.

I took notes as he explained that he'd grown up in LA but that
his parents were from Oklahoma. His dad was Roy I and his
mom was Ruby.

"So you're Roy the Second?"

Throughout our lunch I interrupted with side questions that
often took Roy off track, but sometimes to something more interesting. I was anxious. I knew my time was limited and that
this might be the only time I ever got with my father. I ordered
coffee and dessert, not because I wanted it, but because I wanted
to extend the length of time we had together.

He smiled when he described how supportive his mother was.
How she'd imagined his name in lights just like fellow vibraphonist Lionel Hampton and that she'd eventually seen it. The
story reminded me fondly of my own mother and her support of

me. But there wasn't enough time to move the conversation there. I needed to know more.

He told me the specifics I'd never known about my own racial background: that his dad was Black and mom was half-Cherokee. My mother always mentioned that Roy had some Native American blood, but I'd spent thirty-four years telling people I was half-Black and half-white. Later, when I told my mother, she gave me more info on her grandparents, whom I'd always just known as Jewish. By the end of the day, I would find out that I was three-eighths Black, one-quarter Russian Jewish, one-quarter Romanian Jewish, and one-eighth Native American.

Roy had three sisters: Thomasina, Royena, and Michelé (pronounced mish-ell-Aay). Their names sounded familiar—part of the short list of facts about Roy that my mother had passed down. All were retired LA schoolteachers who looked Native American. He punctuated his statement by pointing to his own cheekbones, then to mine. And in doing so, he continued to confirm that we were related, a fact that wasn't in question, but one for which I could never have too much backup.

Roy was a very physical, animated conversationalist. Even as he sat at a lunch table, his arms waved, his head bobbed, and his face squeezed for emphasis. I saw so much of myself in him, especially his natural, unavoidable smile and gentle chuckles even throughout the serious moments.

He told me that he played two hundred concerts per year, and I nearly spit up my tekka maki. In my world, a band that played one hundred shows a year would be considered extremely hardworking. Two hundred was unheard-of.

"I love performing and I love attention." It felt like looking into a mirror. The way he said it—a statement of fact. The way he felt it, with so much self-assurance. That was who he was. And I had it too. I'd felt it when I joined the Long Winters at a time when my business life had been in a perfect place for me to gracefully retire from music but I couldn't.

He'd married a schoolteacher in 1973 after being together for only three months. I immediately thought of my mother. I wondered what caused him to settle down with his wife and not my mother. But I didn't ask.

Roy and his wife had two children: Mtume, who was thirty-two and lived in North Carolina, and Ayana, who was thirty and lived in New York City. They were both married. I'd heard the names of my half siblings before from my mother but hadn't realized they were so close to me in age—just two and four years younger. They must have been the two little kids I saw standing before me at the school fair in New York all those years ago.

His oldest son Roy III was forty-two and lived in Australia. His mother was Roy's first wife, whom he'd married when they were young, in 1959. Roy III and his mom both appear on the cover of Roy's 1968 album *Stoned Soul Picnic*, posed among a dozen sun-soaked hippies.

"None of the kids play music." This shocked me. How was it that I was so musical and had such a love of music, and most of the people closest to me had none?

I'd been scribbling furiously, making sure to get names and dates while not wasting any time. Then I looked up at Roy. "Are there any more like me?"

His eyes stayed with me as he raised both of his palms out next to his ears and shrugged both shoulders. I took his response as sign language for "I don't know . . . there could be." I also took it as further confirmation that I was his son. Something I'd never been more sure of than at this very moment.

"You know, Alan was in the room when you were conceived."

I was blindsided by this intimate detail, and by the fact that he remembered that night, which I'd always known was during a blackout in New York City. Thinking about my twenty-one-year-old mother having sex was, of course, embarrassing and weird. And thinking of my sweet, nineteen-year-old uncle being in the same room made things worse. My mother would later explain that Alan was asleep, separated by a thick bedspread that acted as a wall.

I explained that I regularly visited New York and that I wanted to meet my half sister, Ayana. For the first time, Roy wasn't confident in his response. He seemed guarded, and he told me that it might take some time. I didn't understand why. He'd just laid out a time line in which I'd been born before he met his wife and started a family. But I let it go, knowing that I now had his phone number and that I'd be in New York often, where both he and Ayana lived.

Roy seemed healthy, but I felt afraid to ask, so I saved it for last. He explained that he and all three of his sisters had health issues, which made me think about my own blood sugar and cholesterol, which had been higher than it should have been for several years, despite exercising and eating well. It was something I'd always been told was a genetic predisposition among African Americans.

"There's no history of cancer." Finally, some good news.

We talked some more about my love of drums and music, the strange combination of growing up in New York and Salt Lake City, the record stores I owned. Then Roy said something that I'd never expected to hear.

"You know, I'm really proud of you." He looked at me, nodding slowly.

"Thanks." It took a little while to process. It initially made me happy—that's the kind of thing you want someone to say to you— a parent, a teacher, a boss. But something inside me felt tentative, and I knew my true reaction wouldn't emerge until long after our lunch.

We both tried to pay the check but he tried harder. Our waiter brought back Roy's credit card, looked at me, smiled, and said, "Thanks, Roy." It gave me a little buzz to feel for the first time that someone had associated me with my father.

Roy said he'd put me on the guest list for the show that night, which I was excited to see—my first Roy Ayers show since the time he opened for the Grateful Dead on that sunny day in Amherst twenty-seven years ago. I knew I wouldn't see him again that night, but I still told him that I'd say hi after the show. More important, I promised to call him about getting in touch with Ayana when I was in New York.

Later that day, after the high of such a good meeting, I began to feel angry over his statement about being proud of me.

It seemed narcissistic. To be proud is to have a feeling of deep pleasure or satisfaction as a result of one's own achievements. Yes, he had helped conceive me. I wouldn't exist without him. But after that point, he'd been nonexistent. I was not his achievement. He should have told me that he was proud of my mother for making the decision to have me the way she did and doing the incredible job she did raising me. Or he should have just said he was proud of himself.

Soon after lunch, when I called Alan to tell him about our meeting, and specifically the comment about being proud of me, he responded perfectly, bringing me back down to earth: "Nabs, Roy is a nice, sweet, extremely talented guy and without him, we wouldn't have you. He was just trying to give you a compliment." As always, Alan offered a calming resolution.

I ARRIVED AT THE TRIPLE DOOR later that evening with the gut feeling that I wouldn't be on Roy's guest list, as promised. I told myself that if I wasn't on the guest list, I'd walk away, still thankful for the time I'd spent with my father earlier in the day. What were my other choices at a sold-out show? Argue and tell someone in the box office that I was his son and they'd better let me in? Call Roy and get voicemail? Call my friend, the promoter at the venue, and tell him my father forgot to put me on his guest list?

"Hi, I'm on Roy's guest list. Nabil." Normally I'd say my full name, but in that instance, it felt weird to say Ayers. It was like the equivalent of saying, "Do you know who I am?" I also wasn't sure if Roy would have put me on the guest list as Nabil Ayers. The clerk pulled out a ticket and a wristband and slid both toward me under the ticket window, explaining that I'd be in the VIP room. I instantly felt relief, realizing at that moment how badly I *did* want to see Roy's performance.

A full wall of glass separated the VIP room from the theater below and offered a perfect view of the stage. The room was warmly decorated, like a hotel suite, with couches and framed art on the walls. Waitstaff came in from time to time to take food and drink orders from the lucky guests, who never had to miss a moment of the show.

I didn't know any of the other people in the VIP room, but they all seemed to know one another, which made me feel uneasy. They were all in their forties and fifties—women in party dresses, men in sport coats. They each appeared to be quite self-important—I overheard one of them say she was a newscaster, but I didn't recognize her.

I'm sure they wondered who I was—the lone person crashing their VIP party. I *really* didn't want to introduce myself, for fear of exposing my lineage and either telling a long story or sulking under the weight of *not* telling one. So I left the room to hang out at the bar until Roy's set began.

When Roy took the stage, the room was energized. I immediately remembered having seen this before as a child in Amherst and having felt the same thing then. His infectious smile, his confident, playful stride. The way his band acted around him—humble and excited to serve. The room was his. Pleasantly surprised facial gestures and quick, agile movements of mallets over his vibes told me that the performer inside his sixty-six-year-old body was still in his twenties.

In a short thirty-minute set, Roy blasted through his greatest hits, including "Everybody Loves the Sunshine." When the audience recognized the song's opening chords and its iconic synth line, everyone jumped to their feet. People swooned. Many of them raised one hand as their bodies began to move. They closed their eyes and shook their heads to the beat, as if attempting to take their bodies somewhere else. The song had always been a meaningful, powerful one for me, and it was exciting to see a room full of people who shared my feelings.

After the show, I didn't attempt to go backstage or wait for Roy outside. Feeling that I'd gotten more than I ever could have hoped for that day, I wanted to quit while I was ahead, so I got in my car, pressed play on my iPod, and drove off smiling, as my seat vibrated to "Everybody Loves the Sunshine."

26.

Love Will Tear Us Apart

Within a few days of meeting my father and seeing him perform, I realized that I wanted more from him. We'd shared an obvious connection. And I'd felt it even more as I watched him onstage—certain moments were like looking into a mirror. When my friends and my mother asked the obvious question, "What's the next step?" it was difficult to admit that I wanted more from Roy. And it was even more difficult to admit it to myself. Why would I risk the tidy, happy ending I'd just orchestrated?

As I thought more about our meeting—how natural and comfortable it had felt, and how easily it had come together—I began to internally question my mother for the first time. She'd set Roy up to fail with her mentions of his self-centeredness and unreliability over the years. But those traits hadn't existed for me. He'd been generous with information; he'd said nice things; he'd showed up. If my mother hadn't instilled in me the lifelong fear that he wouldn't show up, maybe I would have reached out to my father years, even decades, earlier. Maybe we'd have had dozens of lunches by now. Maybe I'd know my half siblings and my aunts. Maybe I'd be excited every time he played in Seattle, instead of clenching my muscles when someone asked about him or hiding out in another city until the date passed.

These thoughts were difficult to grapple with, because it meant opening up feelings about my mother, whose decisions regarding my father I'd always respected, defended, and never questioned. But now I wondered whether my mother had handled things as well as I'd always thought. I'd never been angry with her for choosing to have me and raising me the way she did. I began to question the narrative she'd presented of my father. I wondered whether my mother's own feelings of fear and rejection from Roy had caused her to unnecessarily create those same feelings within me. I knew that she'd had my best interests at heart, but I wished she'd been less protective and that she'd encouraged me to connect with Roy earlier in my adult life.

I called Roy a few times in the months that followed our lunch, but I didn't completely let down my guard—I always had an easy and honest excuse: I'd be visiting New York soon and would love to meet up again. But he was always busy or unavailable, and most of my calls went to voicemail. One day, though, he picked up. I'd been so used to hearing his voicemail that I felt flustered and had to regain my composure.

"Hello?"

"Who is this?" he responded to my greeting as if I'd been a pesky telemarketer.

"It's Nabil," I said slowly, leaving a big blank after my name in which it might have been appropriate to identify myself as his son. But the words wouldn't come out.

Finally understanding who I was, he rushed me along. "Oh yeah, yeah, what's up?" A timer in my head counted down from ten seconds to none as I quickly jumped into my two objectives. "I'm going to be in New York later this week. Can we get together?"

He sounded distracted, like he had a different phone in his other hand on which a caller also wanted something from him. "I'm at the airport right now on my way to Russia."

That was an excuse I hadn't been prepared for. But feeling no room for unimportant questions, I jumped into my next one. "Will Ayana be in town?"

I imagined him at a desk full of messy papers, shuffling them as several people waited anxiously in line for his attention. "I told her about you. Okay, man, I gotta go. Take care."

Click.

Now it was happening to *me*. Now my mother's protective measures were justified, and for the first time, I felt really angry with my father, more than I'd ever been before. But I had no vehicle with which to express my anger. I could *not* call him from now on, but he'd never know—he didn't even know when I *did* call him. I told myself I needed to stop disappointing myself by trying to contact my father and to be happy with the time I got

to spend with him. That was easier to do when I was busy working in Seattle or touring with my band, but more difficult when
I traveled to New York City, which was often.

THE NEXT YEAR, back home in Seattle, I saw an ad for my father's upcoming concert: on October 12, 2007, he'd perform at
Nectar Lounge, a club one block from my apartment. Though
I'd felt frustrated with my inability to connect with him when I
was in New York, I felt optimistic about another Seattle meeting, due to the precedent we'd set at lunch a year earlier.

I called him a couple of weeks before the show to try to schedule some time with him. He answered in a preoccupied state,
sounding like he was driving, reading the newspaper, and getting a pedicure all at once. I explained that I lived near the club
and I invited him and his band to come have dinner at my place
before the show. It felt like the right gesture. My father, with
whom I'd had a recent first-time adult connection, was playing a
block from my home. Dinner there was easier and more flexible
than a restaurant. And it meant more to invite someone into my
home. I hadn't yet thought about what I would have done in my
one-bedroom apartment if he'd brought his full band over for
dinner.

"I've got sound check." He continued to sound anxious and
distracted, to which I replied that I was flexible and only one
block away. "Just come to the show, man. Come to the show. I
gotta run. I'll see you in Seattle."

I felt deflated. What could have been easier? And we'd gotten along so well last time. Was this even more of the unreliability and disappointment my mother warned me about? Then I told myself this wasn't necessarily unreliable or disappointing: it wasn't like he'd committed and then not shown up. He'd been honest. I'd spent years in bands, and I knew it could be hard to plan a dinner on the night of a show. Some musicians, especially singers, don't like to eat even hours before they perform. I thought about every realistic excuse and I sympathized, to a degree.

But I still felt angry and impatient. Over a long lunch just one year earlier, we'd gone from thirty-four years without a connection to an extremely pleasant one. There was no longer anything to fear. Our meeting had been amicable and for me served as a building block for something more, if only more such experiences, once in a while. *What an asshole*, I thought, *for not just saying yes.*

So many of my feelings about my father are connected to his fame and people knowing my connection to him. The kinds of questions I usually field leading up to a Roy Ayers concert? "Are you having dinner with your dad before the show? Are you guys going to hang out? Are you going to jam? Can I be on the guest list? What was it like growing up with him?"

It's always been embarrassing and somewhat humiliating to respond, "I've never really known him, so I don't think we have any plans." I'm usually met with more questions, or a look of sympathy, as if to say, "Oh, sorry I asked about your dead dad."

It stung extra hard this time.

In the past, I'd never asked or expected anything from him. But now I'd both asked and expected something—something

very easy—and I'd been brushed off. Coupled with the distracted, unanswered, and unreturned phone calls, I'd revised our
year-old meeting as a onetime thing. Turns out that meeting was
a stroke of luck for which I was thankful, but it had also placed
me in an uncomfortable, vulnerable position.

ON THE AFTERNOON of the show, the promoter Colin stopped
by my record store, which was also a few blocks from the venue.
Colin was a cool kid in his late twenties who loved hip-hop and
jazz. He fit squarely into the new generation of younger people
who had discovered Roy's music.

"I just talked to Roy! I told him I know you!" Colin told me
excitedly.

"Did he seem like he knew *me*?" I snapped. I immediately felt
bad about my tone, but I didn't feel like justifying it.

Colin seemed taken aback, and didn't answer my question,
which he probably viewed as rhetorical. I was distracted the rest
of the day, aware that my father was around the corner but that
he wouldn't set aside the time to see me.

I moped through dinner with my bandmate Eric and his girlfriend Anna, both good friends whom I needed with me that
night. They knew my whole story with my father, and I explained
to them that I had no plan other than to watch the show and
maybe say hi afterward, if it felt doable. I told myself to expect
very little. But I still found myself hoping for more.

The show was packed with people mostly in their twenties

and thirties, dancing and singing along with my father's songs. On the outskirts of the room were the older, die-hard fans who had been listening to Roy's music and seeing him live for years. While it felt good to see multiple generations in one room—something I didn't see often at concerts—I felt very uncomfortable during the show, like I had a spotlight on me. I was positive that there were people in the room who would say, "Hey, man! We had dinner with your pops before the show. He's such a cool guy!" or, "Hey, man! We're hanging out with your pops after the show. Are you coming?" And I'd have to nod and play along. Or I'd have to tell them my painful truth: my father didn't think of me as important enough to invite.

Roy's band was great, especially the drummer, who looked to be barely in his twenties. Roy was a star as always—engaging, charismatic, and genuine in his delivery. None of that had changed.

But there was a lot about the show that I didn't like. Many of the songs had been reworked. "We Live in Brooklyn, Baby" was a swing instead of the steady, chugging groove that was on the record. "Everybody Loves the Sunshine" was played too fast—deliberately—and as such, it lost its spacey, hypnotic qualities. Roy played on electronic vibes, which made sense for an artist flying to every show, but the plastic pad had significantly less visual impact than the cumbersome yet strong and elegant instrument that Roy had helped make famous in the seventies. I wondered whether I would have noticed all of this if I weren't so frustrated with Roy at that moment.

After the show, the band made its way through the crowd to

the dressing room. I didn't want to say hi. But I also didn't want to stew in my own juices for twenty minutes while Roy cooled down, and then walk into his backstage room, risking rejection—or worse, lack of recognition—in front of his band and my friends. He also might have been going straight to a car. So the time was now. I shoved my way through a few rows of lanky hipsters and grabbed Roy by the shoulder.

"Hey! It's Nabil." I smiled. But I didn't want to.

He grabbed my shoulder back. "Hey, man." He smiled too. But his eyes darted and I immediately knew I'd chosen the wrong time. "Hey, listen, I gotta get going." He never stopped moving as he pointed toward the backstage room. His eyes told me, *I've got places to go and things to do. You understand.*

The fact that I was his son carried no currency. It afforded me no rank over anyone else in the room. I was like one of the fans trying to grab him between his taxi and the club when my mother took me as a child to see him. I removed my hand from his shoulder and let him walk away. Then I turned to find Eric and Anna, whose disappointed faces echoed my own sentiments.

It was the worst I'd felt yet in the yearlong chase to find another moment with my father. I had to muster an incredible amount of courage in order to walk up to him and grab his shoulder—the kind of courage that fuels you further in life because you tried something and you succeeded. It gives you the confidence to take that kind of big, scary, emotional risk again because it was worth it the last time. But when it doesn't work—when it backfires and you're standing in a roomful of people watching your father walk away because he has someplace better to be—it's demoralizing and painful.

Raising a child takes care, time, and energy—things I'd never expected from my father while I was growing up. But on the rare occasion that we, as grown men, were physically in the same room, I expected more than what I got that night.

27.

We Live in Brooklyn, Baby

In 2008, after twenty-six years away from the city I considered home, I moved back to New York. I'd saved money and made a clean break with Seattle, retaining co-ownership of the record store with my partner Jason, but with little involvement in its day-to-day operations. The Long Winters had finished a long tour cycle, and the month before I moved, I tracked all the drum parts for our next record. My plan was to run my own record label, the Control Group, full time for the first time.

I'd recently put out the debut releases by three promising Scandinavian artists: the jittery Danish rock band Figurines, the wide-eyed chanteuse El Perro del Mar, and the burgeoning Swedish pop star Lykke Li. And I'd released the vinyl editions of albums by PJ Harvey, the Killers, and Kings of Leon at a time when the major labels saw no value in releasing vinyl by the artists on their roster. I'd slowly built a catalog of releases that journalists wrote about, DJs played on the radio, and music supervisors placed in TV shows. Figurines had a song featured in *The O.C.*, and videos by El Perro del Mar and Lykke Li got played on MTV. As a result, I started actually selling records—more than I had in any of my own bands before the Long Winters.

The more my label grew, the more I knew I needed to be in New York. I'd landed a deal with the best independent distributor to get my records into stores, and they were based in New York. Schoolyard Heroes, a young Seattle band whose albums I'd released on the Control Group, had signed with Island Records—whose office was in New York—and I was now the band's manager. I was on the phone with someone in New York every day, and I knew from experience how much more I could get done in person. In the past ten years, I'd visited countless times in touring bands, but now I had a true business interest in the city and I felt its pull. I promised myself I'd commit to the Control Group full time for at least one year. Not only would I not look for a job, I wouldn't even entertain one if it landed on me. I would live in the media center of New York without the demands of a record store or a touring band, and I could devote 100 percent of my attention to my label.

Before I left Seattle, I had a dream of what my life in New York would be like:

I was living in a large apartment on Washington Square Park. The living room was glowing with warm light on a crisp autumn evening. Several jovial but mellow people in cozy wool sweaters surrounded a table full of turkey, stuffing, and colorful sides. The guests were all anonymous except for one: my father.

He was standing over the table, placing food on his sturdy white plate in his usual animated fashion, unknowingly bouncing to the song playing in his head. Everyone in the room was focused on him as he told a story that paused often, allowing ample space for chuckles of approval. I found myself starting to feel like a guest. My father turned to me, pointing his spoon as he made eye contact. "You want some turkey?" he asked with genuine concern. But before I could respond, he disappeared to entertain the other guests.

The emotional hangover of this dream was around for several months leading up to my move—enough time for me to analyze the whole thing to death. The easy explanation is I wished I could be together with my father and other family and friends on the most family-focused day of the year. I wanted to be part of a real family, and moving to New York—where my father lived—might afford me that opportunity. But the deeper interpretation—the harder one—was that even in my dreams, my father was leaving me.

No matter how much I might pretend otherwise, my subconscious was letting me know: I wanted Roy in my life. But I wasn't sure how to make that a reality.

ONCE I ARRIVED IN NEW YORK, I found an apartment in Brooklyn. While at that time Seattle's population was less than 10 percent African American, Brooklyn was noticeably different—its population was about one-third African American, with substantial communities of Chinese American, Muslim, Greek American, Latinx, Jewish, Russian American, Caribbean American, and Italian American residents. I quickly found myself at home, in a way I hadn't felt since those days back in North Village.

The feeling of belonging, of home, was most evident to me the morning after Barack Obama was elected president in 2008. That day, my short walk to the subway was interrupted with several pleasant interactions. Some were gentle, passing fist bumps accompanied by a reassuring "yeah, brother." Others were simple nods, denoting a shared bond. All of these were with Black men.

I'll never know if these interactions were reserved for me as a Black man, sharing in the celebration of our newly elected Black president. It's possible that *everyone* on the block that morning—regardless of race or gender—partook in the same exchange. But those fist bumps brought up something that I rarely considered: *These people all see me as Black.*

I thought about it in the context of the man we celebrated: the first *Black* president. It was well-known that Barack Obama was the son of a Black father and a white mother—he and I shared a similar background. His Black wife and Black children solidified his status as a Black man. On the other hand, my mixed, anything-but-Black upbringing prevented me from feeling fully included in any group, Black or white. That morning, while I liked the nods because they meant people thought I belonged, I continued to struggle with the internal conflict that I didn't actually belong . . . completely.

But then I came back to my neighborhood, Fort Greene, a traditionally Black neighborhood in Brooklyn that had recently—while gentrified—become truly diverse; all races mixed and mingled. People referred to it as *Sesame Street*.

In that moment, even though I wasn't sure where I belonged, I somehow felt very much at home.

I'D STARTED REACHING OUT to my half sister Ayana in 2008, soon after I moved to Brooklyn. Roy had remained elusive, but on one quick call he'd finally given me Ayana's email address, allowing me to send an introductory email stating that in my recent meeting with Roy, we'd discovered how much we shared, and I hoped to do the same with her. But she didn't respond. I wondered whether I had the right email address—Roy had read it over the phone, and it contained dashes and seemingly random numbers. But when my Facebook messages were also ignored, I assumed Ayana had chosen not to be in contact with me.

Still, I occasionally wondered at concerts, on the subway, or just walking down the street in my neighborhood if I was standing right next to my half sister without knowing it. I'd grown up never wishing I'd had brothers or sisters. But, in my midthirties, after having my first-ever meaningful conversation with my father, I felt drawn to Ayana, who could tell me more about my father, his family, and possibly about myself.

28.

4 American Dollars

Three months after moving to New York, I ran into Matt, a friend who was the general manager at Beggars Group, the parent company to several respected, powerful independent record labels. We caught up at a bar, sharing life details, and I explained to him my plan to devote myself full time to my own label. We promised to keep in touch.

The next day, Matt emailed asking if I wanted to hear about a new position running one of Beggars Group's labels—4AD—in America.

When I previously envisioned a record company job, I'd always imagined it'd be at a major label. I was working closely with Island Records on Schoolyard Heroes, and Atlantic Records had signed Lykke Li, with whom I was still involved. While

I liked working *with* those large labels, my experiences in my previous bands told me that I didn't want to work *for* them— unlike many independent labels, the majors were too focused on hits. But it hadn't occurred to me that a Beggars label—with which I'd felt connected both musically and ethically—might be an option. Those jobs never opened up, especially a job like running 4AD. I realized how much my vow about moving from Seattle, running my own label, and not looking for a job had accidentally worked in my favor. The confidence with which I'd explained my plan to Matt had likely made me a more attractive candidate than one who was looking for a job.

Two days later, at a coffee shop in SoHo, I met Matt to hear more about the job.

He explained what I already knew from my years at Sonic Boom, where I had worked closely with Beggars. Beggars was owned by one person, Martin Mills. Under Beggars were four completely separate labels: 4AD, Matador Records, Rough Trade Records, and XL Recordings. All of the labels were co-owned by Beggars and the label's original founders, except for 4AD, which was owned wholly by Beggars. A staff of about forty people in New York worked on marketing, radio, press, finance, production, licensing . . . all the functions of a record company. They did so as Beggars employees for each of the individual labels' releases. Matador was the only American label, fully staffed in New York. Of the other London-based labels, both Rough Trade and XL had recently hired dedicated label managers to run their US operations. 4AD was still in the process of looking for someone.

Matt made it clear that it wasn't his decision, but that he thought I'd be a good fit for the job. We left it with my considering his offer to put me in touch with Simon Halliday, who ran 4AD worldwide from London. "He's in New York often, so it would be easy for you guys to meet up," Matt said.

When I walked home from the coffee shop, I have to admit, I was scared. Excited, but scared. I'd just sat with someone who was one step from a label I'd worshipped ever since I first heard Pixies in high school. The label that in college released albums by Cocteau Twins that spoke to me, but in no discernible language. The label that released the Breeders' album *Last Splash*— prompting me to call a radio station to ask what "Cannonball" was the first time I heard it. The label that during my record store days released great albums by the stark, jangly Throwing Muses, New York's noise-turned-elegant Blonde Redhead, and the record-store-clerk-endorsed experimental crooner Scott Walker.

Then there was me, a guy who had played drums in a moderately successful indie band, who had opened a record store with his friend, who had put out some albums by some cool Danes and Swedes, but who knew nothing about running a real record company, let alone *the best* record company. I am not—nor have I ever been—a self-doubting or self-deprecating person. But in that moment, as I walked away from my meeting with Matt, I felt my stomach in my throat. *Doesn't Matt know that I'm not qualified to do this job?* I thought.

Over the next few days I thought through my options, and I began to understand my anxiety. It wasn't that I couldn't run a record label—it was more that I'd never held a real job. I'd washed dishes, installed clunky FOR SALE signs on house lawns, and eventually worked at a record store. And then we opened Sonic Boom and I started the Control Group. I'd managed twenty-three employees, but I'd never worked in an office where I was accountable to people, where people were accountable to me, where I had a boss. At Sonic Boom, we sold thousands of different albums, but here, success or failure was easily measurable by the sale of only a small number of releases each year. All of these factors terrified me, and I wondered whether it would be easier to stick to my original plan: working on the Control Group full time.

One week later, I hadn't yet asked Matt to connect me with Simon. And then my friend Gabe called. Gabe had worked at Sonic Boom for a few years before moving to New York City, where he worked for Vice and now Beggars. "You're *totally fucking this up!*" Gabe barked at me in a gruff, hurried tone. "I hear Matt talking about you. It's *not* what you think. It's not a boring office job. It's great here. People are cool and that job is *the best* job in the building! Call Matt now before they hire someone else!"

There was no room for questions—any I might have had were all answered by Gabe's pep rant, which, despite his intensity, calmed any anxiety I had about going for the job at 4AD.

"IS THERE ANY AMOUNT you *wouldn't* work for?"

Simon Halliday had a unique and charming approach. We'd

just left a long lunch at a Tribeca restaurant that was only a block from my uncle Alan's former Canal Street loft—a part of the city I hadn't seen in decades. Much like our early email exchanges, most of our lunch conversation was not focused on the job at 4AD. Instead, Simon and I had discussed music—we both loved Kraftwerk and Broadcast, whom he'd been heavily involved in signing when he was at Warp Records. Our minimal discussion of the 4AD job was broad. "It's running the campaigns and leading the Beggars staff." Simon seemed less excited when he explained the job's boring details: "It's spending time with the artists and doing some A&R when we're looking at signing someone in America. But a lot of the time, it's just being the guy from 4AD."

Simon spoke with confidence and with the accent of a well-read, highly educated Mancunian who'd spent the eighties at New Order and the Smiths shows and the nineties in London dance clubs. He was five years my senior, and while some of our tastes aligned perfectly, some were completely out of sync: he didn't grow up around much punk or metal, and I didn't grow up around much hip-hop or R&B. But that didn't matter.

I gave him a number, and a few weeks later, I accepted the position as US general manager of 4AD for slightly less than the amount for which I said I wouldn't work.

IN JANUARY 2009, on my first day at 4AD, I asked the woman at the front desk for a pen, and she directed me to the supply closet. I opened the door to find a magical mini-arsenal of pens, pads, paper clips, envelopes, and sticky notes. It was like a disaster preparation kit that ensured that if everyone were trapped in the office for months, we'd still be able to write and staple. At Sonic Boom, Jason or I ordered office supplies and kept nothing more on hand than we absolutely needed. But now, everything was magically at my disposal. That experience gave me my first realization that I had *a real job*. It wasn't the only moment I had that realization.

I'd played in bands for years, on several labels both larger and smaller than 4AD. I owned a record store, and because of that I knew people in every facet of the music business. I'd managed a band on a major label and run my own small label for nearly ten years. But suddenly at 4AD I had twenty-five people who were accountable to me, some of whom had worked in the office for more than a decade; I represented artists I'd loved for years. I'd essentially taken the reverse path of most people. Instead of working for someone else for years, then going out on my own, taking the best parts of what I learned along the way, I'd worked for myself for my entire professional life, and now I suddenly had a boss, in an office, with a closet full of supplies that someone else had stocked.

I felt a touch of imposter syndrome—worrying that people thought I knew what I was doing even though I didn't and assuming that some people didn't have confidence in my abilities.

But those impressions quickly changed.

Beggars was owned by one person, who was accessible and actively involved. It felt closer to Sonic Boom than I expected. I began to grow more assured in my role, which I tried to explain to my mother, who was even more excited about it than me.

"So you find all the new bands?" she asked eagerly over the phone.

"Not exactly," I began to explain. "That's some of it. Though most of my job is running the album campaigns. We have all of these people who each do different things: People who sign the bands and work with them to make the records. People who design and press the CDs and records, and others who sell them to record stores and work with iTunes and other digital stores. Then there's a huge team who works on getting the music reviewed, getting the bands on TV and on the radio, and placing their songs in movies, TV shows, and commercials. There are people who make videos, buy advertising, and of course there's a big accounting office."

"You do all of that!?" My mother's selective listening always works in my favor.

"No, I don't do anything." Then I rephrased. "I *oversee* the people who do all that. I work with them, the bands, their managers, and the UK office, and try to make it all come together seamlessly and effectively. We time things so that we get what we need in the US as far as the band touring, singles and video selection, and timing . . . while balancing that with what the UK and the rest of the world needs."

I hated the analogy that was on the tip of my tongue, but I knew it would land.

"I'm like the conductor of a symphony. The staff is like an orchestra, but you can't just have everyone playing all the time."

. . .

4AD's FIRST THREE RELEASES of 2009 were *Dark Was the Night*, a benefit compilation curated by the National, which raised more than $1 million for AIDS-related charities; Camera Obscura's *My Maudlin Career*; and St. Vincent's *Actor*. We were also starting to talk about the National's anticipated new album, their first since releasing their 2007 breakout album *Boxer*.

I found that after we released those albums, I started to better understand how my company worked: The artists drove everything creative and we backed them up. We offered opinions and sometimes we disagreed with album art, photos, videos, song sequence, and singles choices. But ultimately, the artists made the decisions.

I immediately got to know several artist managers. Some were simply facilitators who booked flights and made sure their artist arrived on time for interviews. Others were more hands on. They had a grand vision and were involved in the music and in long-term, big-picture planning. Many managers existed somewhere between these two extremes.

I also quickly learned that some frustrated managers (and artists) would yell at me when we weren't selling enough records or getting enough radio airplay. Others would hang up on me or threaten me. Once, I was kicked out of a roomful of people.

After my first jarring hang-up, I immediately called Simon, who laughed and told me not to worry—the same person had just hung up on him. It was reassuring to learn that an angry manager or artist never meant I was going to get in trouble with my boss. And it solidified my belief that some people just want to yell—to act out and to be heard and noticed. My job isn't to yell back, it's to help everyone get along and work toward a common goal.

Over time, I became more adept at dealing with these moments, reminding myself of Alan's interaction at Bleecker Bob's. I'd tell myself it wasn't personal and that the yelling manager and I shared the same goal—a successful album. I reminded myself, *This person will calm down when I don't up the ante*. I remembered my own experiences in bands and how frustrating it felt when things didn't go as planned, like my life's dream was slipping through someone else's hands. But now someone else's dreams were partially in *my* hands.

THOUGH THE LONG WINTERS had wound down before I moved from Seattle, we'd agreed to play at Seattle's Bumbershoot festival in the fall of 2009—a year after my move to New York City. I was excited to take a few vacation days to fly back to my former home and play my first show in a year.

But I had reservations too. Not only did the festival include my indie rock band, it also included Roy Ayers, who was scheduled to play the day after us.

After my recent disappointing attempts to connect with my father, I deliberately booked my flight home for the morning after our performance—the morning of my father's. I didn't want to put myself in a position like the last time I'd seen him in Seattle, one in which people might ask me if I could get them into his show or where we were going to dinner afterward. Or worse—since we were both playing the same festival, maybe people would assume we were going to *jam* together. Again, I thought how pathetic that would feel—to be forced to answer with either lies or the brutal truth: we don't have a relationship. *I don't know him.* I didn't want to feel any of that. I wanted to be thousands of miles away, back home in New York, when he was onstage in Seattle.

OUR SHOW WAS PACKED, nostalgic, fun, and everything it should have been. But I felt that a small part of it had been stolen by my father. I allowed him—through no fault of his own—to take away my ability to completely relax and enjoy myself in my own space.

29.

Seasons Change

By the end of 2011, I'd been at 4AD for nearly three years, and I'd found my stride. We'd had many successes: The National's *High Violet* album debuted at number three on the Billboard album charts, selling more than fifty thousand copies in its first week in the United States—the highest first-week US sales and chart position for 4AD to date. Deerhunter's *Halcyon Digest*—our first album working with the band in America— remains their bestselling and most highly praised album to date. Tune-Yards, essentially the singer and multi-instrumentalist Merrill Garbus, whom we'd signed as a fiercely independent solo artist with one of the most powerful voices on earth, surprised us with *whokill*, a still-divisive album that broke down barriers, got her on national TV, and earned the number one position on the *Village Voice* music critics poll that year. I felt especially close to Tune-Yards, having traveled all over the country to help sign Merrill. The Big Pink sold more than forty thousand albums in the US, no small feat at the time for a debut album by a British band. And we were preparing to release *Visions*, our first album with the Canadian producer and singer known as Grimes.

I traveled every few months to 4AD's headquarters in London, which, like our New York office, was filled with music fans, many of whom had started their careers in bands or record stores, like me. I stayed at the K West Hotel, a notorious rock star destination where I spent one late night at the rowdy hotel bar discussing Van Halen with Pantera's now deceased drummer Vinnie Paul. I was used to meeting famous musicians, but not cowboy hat–wearing metal drummers.

LATER THAT YEAR, at California's Coachella Valley Music and Arts Festival, an electronic-chipped laminate separated me from the sun-drenched one-hundred-thousand-person crowd. I'd been backstage at hundreds of shows but never someplace this nice, where a spacious, comfortable village lived in seclusion behind the gigantic main stage. Backstage at Coachella looked like a movie set where sleek machines gently sprayed mists of cool water, and palm trees protected me from the sun. As I tipped back my ice-cold container of free coconut water, I remembered my day at Lollapalooza during college when my friends and I walked for two hours in the rain to see Jane's Addiction, unaware that backstage, a select few were living in the lap of luxury.

My laminate allowed me side-stage access during every performance except for Kanye West's, where instead of a cluster of rock stars and industry colleagues, I met one large bouncer who stood next to a sign that read NO LAMINATES. At another stage I found myself standing next to Katy Perry, who appeared to be enraptured by Robyn's live set. A few hours later during PJ Harvey's set, I turned to find Robyn standing behind me hiding in a hoodie. It reminded me of the many musicians who bought music at Sonic Boom and Easy Street, as well as the people I worked with—there were still people in the music business who were, at their core, simply music fans.

THE MORE I INTERACTED WITH artists both big and small, the more I realized how much I had in common with them. When I was in bands, I wanted to know that my record label was working in my best interest. Now, as the head of a record label, I wanted to impart that feeling to the artists. Selling fifty thousand albums by the National in one week was exhilarating, but I was equally fulfilled by landing a song in a worldwide car commercial for the relatively obscure Danish band Efterklang, or by simply listening to the very rough home recording of what would become Tune-Yards' biggest song to date, "Water Fountain." I loved being part of the process and reinforcing to our staff that the victories for the smaller artists were just as important as they were for our bigger artists.

The early 2010s was a peak time for independent labels to break through to a greater portion of the mainstream. Our goal was never to reach *everyone*—the music we release is still too good for that. But we were always pushing to reach a wider audience for our artists, and more tools and mechanisms than ever were at our disposal. Independent record stores were selling huge amounts of vinyl to new buyers, and at the opposite end of the spectrum, iTunes made it easy to connect fans to albums with a single click. Noncommercial and college radio stations that had traditionally supported underground music with small, local broadcast signals were now online and available to stream worldwide. We were able to more precisely target buyers with digital advertising. Many journalists and gatekeepers who placed music in film and TV spots were now of my generation—they understood and liked the music we released, and they had the power to help push it forward.

With the Control Group, I always assumed there was a secret that all the great labels kept—that they could push a special button and make things work for an artist or album. That's what it looked like from the outside. But once I was on the inside, I realized there was no such magic bullet. When things worked well, it was because the artist had a great vision and made an album that connected with people—almost always with one song as an entry point. From there, having an office full of smart, creative, connected, motivated people was essential. And giving those people authority and budgets to spend in the right place at the right time helped even more. Good luck always helped too.

. . .

IN 2014 I EXPERIENCED a lightning moment when the Baltimore band Future Islands performed on *The Late Show with David Letterman*. Many of our artists played on TV, which rarely made an impact on sales. It was a talking point that helped us frame an artist as big or important, but the performance itself—which was always the last spot on the program—was often a costly, elaborate affair, and we were expected to pay for flights, hotels, gear rental, crew, extra lighting, a string section, dancers . . . whatever an artist felt they needed to create a lightning moment.

Future Islands needed no bells and whistles when they played *Letterman*. We were preparing to release the band's fourth album and their first on 4AD, *Singles*. They'd already played hundreds of live shows in their career, and when our publicist secured the *Letterman* offer, the band reluctantly canceled one show to make it work. That day the band pulled their van up to the Ed Sullivan Theater, the same venue where the Beatles made their American debut fifty years earlier, and loaded in their gear as they would have at any show. They wore the same clothes they would have worn on any other night. And in four short minutes, they completely altered their own trajectory—and the next day, the internet.

Future Islands often played ten or more nights in a row without a night off. To them, *Letterman* was just another show. The stage was theirs, and when the four-on-the-floor beat of "Seasons (Waiting on You)" pulsed under a melodic bassline and floating synths, four normal-looking guys came into view.

The singer Sam Herring wore a tucked-in black T-shirt and moved nervously before releasing the song's opening lyrics, "Seasons change . . . and I tried hard just to soften you." Sam's voice was gruff and soulful, and his delivery wasn't contrived as many singers' can be on TV—it was passionately heartfelt and honest. His eyes radiated sympathy, and as the song progressed, Sam's movements evolved into a dance. His head bobbed as he crouched down low, his knees wobbling in time. Sam's intensity escalated as the song built. He pounded his chest so hard that the thump of his fist could be heard over the music. He growled a guttural version of the normally sweet chorus and licked his fingers to emphasize the word "taste." I'd attended many TV performances, but just two minutes into this one, my colleagues and I looked at each other, aware that we were witnessing something rare: a very emotional and powerful TV performance.

It wasn't unusual to run into David Letterman after the show—he'd once nodded to me as he breezed by in long, silk-like basketball shorts. And it was common to see major stars in the narrow hallways and cramped elevators backstage at TV studios—once I'd nearly tripped into Alec Baldwin as he stretched just before his segment with Jimmy Fallon. Fallon's backstage was larger and more social than Letterman's, and once at a St. Vincent taping I was able to see Serena Williams, Blake Shelton, Questlove, and Elvis Costello without turning my head. But I'd never run into Letterman's animated band leader, Paul Shaffer, whom I couldn't help but see as Artie Fufkin, the smarmy record company man he played in *This Is Spinal Tap*.

That night, though, *I* was the Artie Fufkin shaking Paul's

hand as he congratulated me as if I myself had just played in Future Islands. He responded enthusiastically to my suggestion that he sit in on keyboards the next time Future Islands performed on the show—something he was known to do from time to time. While that didn't exactly come to pass, Paul did sing backup vocals with Future Islands when they returned to *Letterman* one year later. I would have shared my Paul Schaffer interaction with the band over celebratory drinks or dinner, but they had to get on the road immediately—the next night's gig was seven hundred miles away in Asheville, North Carolina.

The next morning our publicist received a thank-you email from the *Letterman* booker, which rarely happened. The Future Islands *Letterman* YouTube clip quickly racked up millions of views—an amount that dwarfed previous performances by superstar acts—and it was shared and talked about by everyone from Bono to the Foo Fighters. It helped Future Islands to land slots at festivals around the world and helped us to make *Singles* the band's most successful album to date.

Though many of our artists were excellent live, I wouldn't again witness a TV performance that powerful until Big Thief performed in the same venue on *The Late Show with Stephen Colbert* in 2019. It worked for the same reason Future Islands' performance did: Big Thief was an amazing band that played without pretense and without bells and whistles. The band's singer and guitarist Adrianne Lenker faced inward toward her bandmates, who appeared to play for each other, not the audience. The song ended with a noisy, cut-off guitar solo that felt nothing like a traditional television performance. Big Thief wanted to connect with people, but more than that, they wanted to connect with one another.

FEW MOMENTS WERE MORE EXCITING than these—when something clicked and the dominoes began to fall: when a great live show helped an artist to get a TV booking, which helped to get more press, which helped to get more radio, which triggered the need to ship more records and spend more on advertising, which always prompted the question "How can we get the song in a commercial?" When things were firing on all cylinders, we were several months ahead, talking about the next single, the next tour, or how to best capture year-end attention. It reminded me of my happiest moments playing in a band but even more so—I had more control and input and I felt 100 percent informed.

As a teenager who ran legal documents around New York City all summer, I'd made myself a promise: I wanted to be a boss, but not the kind who treated others like shit. And I wanted to work with talented people whom I liked and respected. I'd achieved this at Sonic Boom, but I soon realized at 4AD, I'd established my life just as I'd planned back then: somewhere between the street and the upstairs. We did millions of dollars of business each year and contributed to the success of vital, groundbreaking artists. And I did my part in a T-shirt and jeans, beginning around ten o'clock each morning, surrounded by talented people whom I genuinely liked and respected.

. . .

WE DIDN'T SIGN many new artists at 4AD, only about two per year on average. While it wasn't my job to find new artists, I was often involved in the signing process. Many of the artists we wanted to work with also had interest from other labels—remarkable independent labels smaller than ours, our direct competitors, and major labels who had signed artists like the Shins, Arcade Fire, and TV on the Radio after their success on indie labels. Part of my job was to meet prospective artists and managers and explain how our American office worked and how it could work for them.

Every now and then, my father would come up in these meetings.

Over tacos in Austin, one member of the Florida post-punk band Merchandise began singing "Everybody Loves the Sunshine" to me, while his bandmates watched, obviously unfamiliar with the song.

The eccentric London singer-songwriter James Canty—after a few drinks at the Ear Inn, a three-minute walk from 501 Canal—admitted that he'd finally worked up the nerve to broach the subject: "Is Roy Ayers your father?"

Whenever this happened, I assumed people thought, *Oh, that's how you got your job.* And I felt the need to backpedal and share my non-relationship with my father, primarily to demonstrate that he'd had zero influence over my career.

It wasn't until we were courting the New York musician Twin

Shadow that things changed. In our office one afternoon, he mentioned cautiously and politely that he'd heard that Roy Ayers was my father, and allowed space for me to explain that while he was, I didn't know him at all, and that I'd recently been trying to get in touch with his daughter—my half sister—who lived in New York. Then his manager chimed in. "Oh, I know Yanni." The room felt still and awkward, and I quickly changed the subject, sinking under the fact that something raw and personal had just been exposed. This person I'd just met—in a work setting— had casually dropped the nickname of my half sister Ayana, whom I'd never met, despite my attempts, despite her proximity.

30.

Alkebu-Lan

Further attempts to contact my father had been futile, but once, about six months after our disappointing run-in at his concert in Seattle, I woke up to a voicemail from him. It was a simple, casual message in which he spoke slowly and thoughtfully.

"Hey, Nabil. It's Roy. I'm just calling to say I'm thinking about you. Okay. Take care."

I knew my father was aging, and his voicemail immediately made me search his name online for fear something had happened. His voice contained a somber tone, and his message sounded incomplete—like it was missing some closing words like "call me back" or "I hope you're doing well." I wondered what he'd actually been thinking—what had caused him to call me of his own volition for the first time in his life. For a moment I felt sorry for him. His guard was audibly down and he'd demonstrated vulnerability.

Then my emotions shifted. Maybe instead his message was a selfish act, one that existed to make himself feel better. It certainly lacked any consideration that it might unnecessarily string me along and offer more false hope.

While my father had at least left me one voicemail, Ayana had completely ignored every attempt I'd made to contact her.

MY FATHER'S REAL FAMILY, as I call it, consists of the two children he had with his current wife, Ayana and her brother Mtume. After my last unsuccessful attempt to contact Ayana, I explained my story to a friend, who encouraged me to reach out to Mtume. I sent Mtume the same message via Facebook that I'd sent Ayana over the years, in which I explained our shared connection and my wish to be in touch. I made it clear that I existed before our father's current marriage, and that I was a successful adult who wasn't after anything.

Two days later, Mtume replied, agreeing to meet sometime.

It was true I didn't want or need anything from him: I simply wanted to connect and see where it went. I couldn't share stories about our father because I didn't have any to share. Meeting Mtume was a research project on my own existence. I wondered whether he'd be able to tell me more about our family and our father's medical history. I wondered whether we'd look alike and if I'd notice shared mannerisms as I had in our father. The goal wasn't to gain a brother, it was to gain information.

A few months later, I attended a bachelor party in North Carolina, two hours from Raleigh, where Mtume lived with his family. Again fearing rejection or silence, I messaged Mtume, explaining that I'd be nearby and could easily come meet him. He responded quickly and we made a plan to meet for lunch.

On the flight to North Carolina, my friend Robby had introduced me to the Miles Davis album *On the Corner*. I was familiar with its cartoonish yellow cover but not with the music, which sounded less like jazz and more like experimental rock. That day, on my solo drive to meet Mtume in Raleigh, I listened to *On the Corner* twice through. Miles's trumpet was often up front, as were the guitars, but the consistent thread of the album was the skittering drumming and percussion. *On the Corner* is a rhythmic masterpiece, and a perfect driving album that felt important, safe, and connective on my journey.

Along with Miles, navigation prompts soundtracked my drive through Raleigh, where wide, tree-lined boulevards competed for cleanliness. I stuck to the speed limit, afraid of being pulled over in the South, until I reached my destination: a beautiful house, built to look colonial with brick and white trim.

After I knocked on the front door, I adjusted my glasses and ran my hands down my shirt to smooth out any wrinkles from the drive. Mtume opened the heavy white door and revealed himself to look . . . not much like me. Had I been randomly next to him someplace, neither of us would have given each other a second look. He was built like a football player—stocky and at least an inch taller than me. We shared our father's thinning hairline and high cheekbones, but Mtume's nose was wider than mine and his skin was darker. We both smiled and I introduced myself in the voice that I hate—the one that sounds like I want something. We hugged—separated by a handshake—and Mtume warmly welcomed me into his home.

Before we left for lunch, I met his wife and seven-year-old daughter, my niece, whose smiles demonstrated that their excitement to meet me was greater than Mtume's. He later revealed that his wife—after seeing my picture—told him he *had* to meet me.

Over a lunch of burgers in a suburban restaurant, I discovered how little Mtume and I have in common: he loves sports and runs a car dealership. He's never played music, while our father and I have built our lives and careers around music. When I asked about his name, Mtume explained that he was named after the musician James Mtume, his godfather, who was good friends with our father.

Mtume seemed unfazed by my origin story and mentioned that our grandfather had "a family on the side." I took that as his way of justifying our father's behavior in the seventies. When I mentioned my failed attempts to reach Ayana, Mtume told me that his sister was very protective of their mother and that he wasn't surprised that she hadn't responded to me. For the first time, I thought about Ayana in the context of my mother, and how protective I'd be if someone tried to suddenly intrude into our lives.

Then, to my surprise, he informed me about another sister of ours, who had recently been in contact with him via Facebook but whom I hadn't been aware of, Eboni. She lived in Philadelphia and had a story similar to mine. Mtume hadn't yet replied to Eboni's messages, but I was immediately fascinated with anyone who claimed to be related and wanted to connect. Mtume agreed to share Eboni's contact information.

When I arrived back at the bachelor party that evening, my friends clammed up and feigned sobriety, as if I'd returned from a funeral and they didn't want to be seen having fun. I allowed them to relax, telling them that it had been a worthwhile, interesting meeting but in no way had it been life altering. I hadn't gained a brother but I'd learned a lot more about my father's family. And I knew about Eboni, whom I would hopefully reach soon.

On the drive to the airport, I played *On the Corner* again and looked up the album to learn more about it. Toward the bottom of the credits, the percussionist is credited as James Mtume, the musician my half brother is named after.

"I WAS ALSO BORN in 1972! LOL, Roy was busy!"

Eboni's response to my first Facebook message was encouraging. Only a few weeks after we messaged, we met in person at a Philadelphia restaurant near her home, where she lived with her two sons—my nephews.

"I feel weird saying this," I told Eboni, "but I've always thought about our father's funeral—when he eventually dies.

I've wondered whether I'd go and who I'd go with. And now I think I would definitely want to go with you."

"I can't believe you said that," Eboni replied. "I've had the same thought about his funeral. And yes, I will go with you."

It felt dark, but also fitting that the first plan we'd made together, forty-four years into our lives, was to attend our father's funeral. While he was still alive and well, we both silently knew that his funeral would likely be the next time we saw him.

I had a strangely easy time unloading my thoughts on Eboni, thoughts I'd been holding on to for most of my life. Though our first in-person conversation had begun with small talk about the menu, it quickly shifted to Roy and the background we'd unknowingly had in common for over forty years.

As we talked, I tried to see myself in Eboni. While we have the same father, our mothers come from different backgrounds. Eboni's mother Verrona is Black, and my mother is white. But our mothers' similarities are more compelling than their differences. They had a child with the same man—in the same year—when they were twenty-two and single. And they both knew that their child would be born and raised without a biological father.

I felt an immediate bond with Eboni even before we met. Ayana and Mtume felt like people I should meet, but Eboni felt like someone I *wanted* to meet, which carried more weight, probably because her excitement matched my own.

Like me, Eboni has never known our father and has had several brief, disappointing interactions with him. She shared a relatable story about herself as a teenager sneaking backstage at a festival to see our father perform. When she made eye contact, she could see that Roy recognized her, but he showed no reaction. Their eyes locked until he turned away and went on with his busy schedule. It was painful to hear someone else recount something similar to my own experiences with the same person. I felt bad for Eboni, and for the first time in my life, I understood why people's faces turned the way they did when I told them my stories about my father.

Not long into our conversation, Eboni showed me a photograph. "This is my dad . . . our dad," she corrected herself. "And my mom, and some other cool folks I don't know, in Cleveland." I held the photo, studying our father's features. I'd seen many photos of him, some that looked a lot like me, but never as much as this one. He'd been in his early thirties when the picture was taken—a handwritten date on the back read February 1972, a date that caused me to laugh.

"So I was born in January 1972," I explained. "This picture was taken a month later, when he was passing through Cleveland, where your mom drove from Pittsburgh to see him. And you were born in December." I smiled at Eboni, intimating that this photo might have been taken on the night she was conceived.

In the photograph, my father is in the center—both physically and metaphorically—closely flanked by two gorgeous young women and two cool, handsome men on the outside. Vests, Afros, and wide collars indicate the era, but nothing lends as much authenticity to the scene as the long drinks, clear glass ashtray, and two packs of Kool cigarettes that appear to have been perfectly crumpled by a set designer. The picture looks too good to possibly be real.

As I stared at the photograph, I tried to get inside my father's head. He was confident, but not arrogant. It was *his* table and he was with *his* people, but like my experience at Electric Lady Studios, I could see that he needed and respected those people. And they worshipped him, but in a mutually respectful way. My father's half smile looked so much like mine that it made me self-conscious: *Is this how people see me? Do I seem smug and arrogant? Or confident and welcoming?*

On the train home to New York that day, I thought about my father's children. I recited our names, considering the coincidence that four different women had produced five different children with him and that after Roy III, each of us had been given unusual, five-letter names: Nabil, Eboni, Ayana, Mtume.

I studied the rhythm of our names—they each contained three syllables except mine. I wondered whether there were more children like me and Eboni, and if they also had five-letter names.

31.

You Got a Little Soul
in You I See

In 2015, when I needed to refinance my Brooklyn apartment, my gregarious, proudly Greek mortgage broker emailed me requesting information for the loan application:

> Also, filling out the personal data . . . what are you? I can't figure it out. You got a little soul in you I see . . . Not white . . . what do you pick on government monitoring stuff. I'm guessing maybe middle eastern? Black? There are shit ton of picks online. You really make it challenging. LOL. I know we are cool so I can ask you this bluntly. I put down white last time but not sure I really nailed that one. LOL.

At that moment, my race was the only thing standing between me and a six-figure loan. I considered what might be the best answer—which answer might be right or wrong, and how it could positively or negatively affect my life. In retrospect, ticking the African American box on my college application had presumably helped. And ticking the white box on that Sonic Boom Records loan application had seemingly not helped. But for this loan, there wasn't a box to tick, just an open-ended email to which I could answer however I wanted. For the first time, I truly got to choose who I was. *What* I was. I was a mix of races, and my broker's email allowed me to say exactly that. I decided I'd match his casual demeanor, and I replied:

Black / white / whatever will get me the best interest rate.

EVEN THOUGH I was well established in New York and at 4AD, my online dating experiments were failing. None got as far as an online conversation, let alone a date. I was surprised to find that one dating app offered filters for race. My face crinkled as I considered my options—Indian, Chinese, African American . . . It felt more like a food delivery app. But when I considered that these were actual human traits—attached to real people, I just chose the most obvious one: *All*. I occasionally opened the app and scrolled through smiling faces, but I was always distracted by the notion that I could choose, or *not choose* a particular race. I never Liked or contacted anyone.

Luckily for me, many of my friends in New York wanted to set me up with their single friends, launching a series of my first-ever blind dates. I had drinks with an artfully tattooed graphic designer and dinner with a famous ballet dancer, after which my mother expressed not the happiness I expected, but rather concern over the possible eating disorders I'd have to live with if we decided to spend the rest of our lives together after just one date. I went out with an ER doctor who, in our first five minutes, chugged a martini and told me to never do cocaine after forty, something that had no bearing on my life but terrified some of my colleagues when I shared the doctor's advice.

These women all had something in common: they were white. Before I met them, I knew they would be white because none of my friends had mentioned their race. White was the default. Race needed to be mentioned only if it was other than white, a safeguard in case I had a problem dating someone who was not white.

I quickly found that dating was bringing issues of race to the forefront in my life, in a way few other moments had. And I became fascinated with the internal dialogue that this series of assumptions—of non-discussions—had created.

My friends all know that I'm half-Black, so it stands to reason that Black would *also* be a default dating group for me. Yet each time they set me up, I wondered whether they would mention that my date would be white, to make sure my Black side was okay with it. They didn't. Did they not because my friends doing the matchmaking were also white? Did they not because they didn't see me as Black? I wonder how they described me to my prospective dates. "He's Black but not really. He's not that Black. He's kind of mixed."

A friend offered to set me up with someone she described as

"a beautiful Indian woman." As great as she sounded, I wondered why my friend had to point out the woman's race—why her heritage was important. Was it to give me the opportunity to say, "Oh, sorry, I don't like Brown women"?

Another friend once offered to set me up. "She's really great. She went to Columbia. She loves music. Oh, do you like Black women?"

"Yes, I like *all* Black women. *Every single one*," I said, a little peeved.

That day, my friend unfortunately bore the brunt of the many conversations I'd patiently lived through before ours, conversations that were increasingly offending me. I've seen women of every race that I find attractive and *un*attractive. It's never because of their race. So how could I be expected to answer the "do you like . . ." question? I quickly inferred that the real question was "Do you *dislike* Black women?" But it sounds better framed in the positive, a seemingly inoffensive question that welcomed a seemingly inoffensive answer.

These experiences made me consider how people viewed me. As a child, it came out when people asked me if I was poor or if I was adopted. Later, when I was touring in bands, people asked more blunt and pointed questions like "Where are you from?" or the classic "What are you?" But now, as an adult approaching middle age and living in a large, cosmopolitan city, I didn't think anyone cared about my race. It turns out that people thought about it more than I knew.

A few years later, I married the most beautiful, wonderful woman I've ever met. I have to admit, I pondered her racial background on that night. And she later admitted that she wondered about mine as well. We were introduced at a wedding, where there were no filters to adjust or boxes to tick. And I remember how refreshing it felt, as we sipped our cocktails and chatted, to not know—to not have been forewarned, to have made no choice—to simply enjoy our connection.

IN EARLY 2016, Jason and I decided to sell Sonic Boom Records. He continued to run the store after I moved to New York, but he and his wife now had two children, and they wanted to move to Minneapolis to be closer to family. We sold Sonic Boom to a customer, which was the perfect outcome. I'd recently started writing for fun in my free time, and I'd cataloged dozens of stories from the early days of the store. When we discussed how to announce the Sonic Boom sale, I suggested that I write a short piece looking back on the store's history to go alongside the announcement in Seattle's independent alternative weekly *The Stranger*. When Sean Nelson—*The Stranger*'s arts editor and former singer in Harvey Danger—agreed to run my piece, I became a published writer for the first time. Turns out I liked writing as much as I liked playing music.

Next, I wrote a piece on my racial identity for New York's Black culture website *The Root*. And soon after that, a piece for *HuffPost* on the shocking history of the Ku Klux Klan I discovered while visiting Dallas, Texas.

Even though I hadn't worked day to day at Sonic Boom for several years, and the sale of the store made sense, it still felt like the end of an era for me. I was thrilled to be the guy from 4AD, but now I was *only* the guy from 4AD. Luckily for me, writing filled that empty space and became a new and powerful way for me to say things that were—out of nowhere—begging to come out.

32.

Oh God Guide Me

I 'd been to Chicago several times since moving to New York, but while visiting for work in the fall of 2017, I finally made a plan to stop by a place I'd always wanted to work into my schedule: the Baha'i House of Worship in nearby Wilmette, Illinois. Opened in 1953 after fifty years of construction, it's the oldest standing Baha'i house of worship in the world—one that serves as an international destination for Baha'is and people of all faiths. I knew that my mother and Alan had once driven to Chicago to attend a Baha'i convention before I was born, and I was excited to finally make the trip.

When the taxi dropped me off in front of the grounds, a sign, carved into a thick wall of granite, greeted me:

THE BAHA'I HOUSE OF WORSHIP

Walking up the twenty or so steps to the magnificent structure, I felt its presence grow larger as I drew closer. Toward the
top, I felt slightly winded—not from the exercise, but from the
wave of energy that quietly engulfed me as I approached. I am
not a religious person, but standing in the shadow of this building was a weighty experience.

Even on a cloudy day, the building pulled in powerful light
through its hundreds of windows. Three lone visitors sat nowhere
near one another, occupying just a few of what must have been a
thousand chairs, and I noticed how different they looked—like
tourists from three different countries and three different generations. Then I remembered the magic of the Baha'i Faith. These
people could have all been at any of the parties I attended as a
child; the frail, elderly Asian man, the middle-aged, heavyset
Black woman, and the bespectacled white man in his twenties
might have been separated by race, but they were united by faith.

I sat in the temple for twenty minutes, reading literature, staring up at the dome and its incredible architecture, and just
thinking—about my name, my mother, and my connection to this
place.

Afterward, I checked out the bookstore, perusing shelves of
books that contained words and phrases I recognized: Bahá'u'lláh,
the *Báb*, and 'Abdu'l-Bahá. They all awakened memories of childhood events.

In the back corner, there was a shelf of identical green hard-
cover books with gold embossed spines. Even though I hadn't seen
a copy since I was a child, I recognized them immediately: *The*

Dawn-Breakers: Nabil's Narrative. I held the heavy, encyclopedia-like book and ran my hand over its textured letters. I'd assumed *Nabil's Narrative* was as rare as my name felt—I'd never seen another copy of the book anywhere. But seeing a Costco-sized quantity on a shelf in Chicago reminded me exactly where I was. I hadn't expected to feel so connected to a place I'd never been, but the Baha'i Faith was still very much ingrained in me.

I left feeling satisfied and connected, as if I'd returned to a childhood home. Words and, more than anything, feelings of complete peace and unity had drawn me in. Even though I'd never seen this structure before, it had put me in an extremely familiar place: open, thankful, and happy.

THAT DAY, IN THE TAXI to O'Hare Airport, I reflected upon my great life. I thought about my girlfriend, to whom I would soon propose marriage. I focused on my good health, my supportive and encouraging friends, my exciting job, and all of the other wonderful things in my life.

Then my thoughts turned to my father, which caused my smile to fade. He had no connection to the Baha'i Faith. But much like the Baha'i Faith, he'd been a constant presence in my life each time I saw his albums in a record store or his name in a club listing, each time I heard his song in a bar.

The Baha'i Faith had never disappointed me like my father had. It had never caused me to feel regretful, embarrassed, frustrated, or lonely. If I'd ever tried to approach the Baha'i Faith in my adult life—as I had my father—I knew it would be there to welcome me, to connect me to people, to comfort and guide me.

My attempts to contact my father had been scattershot and unfocused, and I still didn't know what I'd hoped to gain. It felt more like an exercise in ego satisfaction than a true effort to connect. I was angry when he hadn't returned my calls. But if he had, where would it have gone? When I'd finally gotten close enough to my father—after our failed second meeting at his Seattle concert—it'd left a bitter taste in my mouth. I'd left angry, and that feeling had remained and overtaken the many years that I now viewed as blissful ignorance.

Why, I thought as the taxi approached the airport, *can't my father be part of the greatness in my life?*

Right then, the confluence of these feelings—disconnectedness from and anger toward my father, and renewed connection to the Baha'i Faith, made me wonder for the first time who I really was. Not in a way that made me feel lost or unhappy. Rather, I felt a swirling, kinetic energy—a powerful, intangible force that surrounded me and demanded to find out more about where I'd come from. I'd only known a few things about my father's family. Suddenly, I desperately needed to know more, and I felt less sure than ever that I'd get any information from my father.

It was in that place, at that moment, that I decided to take a DNA test.

33.

Roots Deep in Slavery

On a clear, chilly day in the winter of 2017, I sent ninety-nine dollars and a tiny tube of my saliva to the genetic testing company 23andMe, curious about what the results would tell me. My mother was fairly certain of her background: Eastern European Jewish. She's always been diligent about keeping in touch with her many cousins and continues to find new ones. They're wonderful people, and I'm always happy to see them at family gatherings. I also take them for granted: It's easy. They've always existed.

But while I'd recently met Mtume and Eboni, neither of them had offered much of my father's family history. By sending my DNA to 23andMe, I hoped to learn something more—anything more—about my father's side of my family.

A month later, I got an email full of pie charts and graphics neatly breaking down my identity. According to 23andMe, I was 66.2 percent European—which includes 51 percent Ashkenazi Jewish—and 32.6 percent sub-Saharan African. During our lunch in Seattle, my father had pointed to both of our cheekbones and attributed them to his one-quarter Native American heritage. But my DNA results claimed I was 0.3 percent Native American—a tiny fraction. These numbers didn't change who I'd always been, but they suggested that my father's ancestry might be less straight-forward than I thought. After seeing my results, I felt less Black than ever.

I'd opted in to 23andMe's communication system, which al-lows newly found DNA relatives to establish contact within the site. Before I had a chance to explore it, a distant cousin on my father's side messaged me. We exchanged information and a cou-ple of weeks later, I awoke to an email from him with an attach-ment titled Ayers Family Tree. Instead of going into work that morning, I made a pot of coffee and stayed on the couch, scrolling through the document's twenty-plus pages of photographs and dense text. I saw dozens of names—Winnie, Luvenia, Moses—none that I recognized.

Then I saw Ruby, my father's mother's name. Below Ruby, my father and his three sisters—Thomasina, Royena, and Michelé. Below my father, his oldest son Roy III—his only child when the family tree was written in 1963.

I know I'm lucky to have known my mother's parents and even her grandfather—my great-grandfather. Knowing those people allowed me to discover that my mother laughs with her whole body, just like her grandfather, and that, like her mother, she waves her hand as if to physically push away uncomfortable conversation. Because of those relationships, I'm able to see pieces of my mother's family in myself.

With this family tree, for the first time, I was connected to my paternal ancestors. I read their stories and studied their photographs, searching for features in common with my own.

The author Samuel L. Ayers was my great-granduncle—the brother of my paternal great-grandfather James Ayers—born in 1898. After a brief introduction, he asserted:

> *Ayers is an English name.*
> *I don't know how this happened or where he came from, but Isaac Ayers, my grandfather, was a slave owned by Dr. Ayers of Ashland, Mississippi in Benton County.*

Even though I'd always assumed that my paternal ancestors were enslaved, to have it confirmed—that Isaac Ayers, my great-great-great-grandfather, was born into slavery around 1825—brought it much closer to home. I imagined Isaac, a man who might have looked like me and my father, with darker skin. Maybe he had a strong, stoic stare, not sharing my and Roy's automatic smile. To read the name of the enslaver—a doctor, an educated man—made me feel sick to my stomach. I felt winded when I thought about how I'd chosen my last name because of my father, knowing now that Ayers was a name that someone in my family had been given only when stripped of their own name, in order to demonstrate ownership.

I continued to read.

When the Emancipation Proclamation was signed in 1863, Dr. Ayers ordered his slaves to continue their services as they had formerly. My grandfather, who was very vocal and spokesman for the group replied, "Look here, aren't we free?" He was told emphatically by Dr. Ayers, "No, you are NOT free!" They had no money or means of transportation so they remained on Dr. Ayers' farm as sharecroppers until they could accumulate enough to leave . . . although there was really nowhere to go.

Isaac's son, James William Ayers, was born in 1850 and worked on a plantation for the first twenty years of his life, though he was technically free for the last seven of those years.

His wife, my great-great-aunt, Jenny Elizabeth Ayers, had been sold away from her family in Texas as a child and brought to Benton County. She had ankle scars from the bloodhounds that chased runaway enslaved people. She later had fifteen children. I pondered Jenny Elizabeth's life while thinking about Roy's sister, Thomasina Ayers Pleasant, a strong-looking woman with a sharp smile and a striking head of reddish-black hair. Only three generations after Jenny, Thomasina had earned her undergraduate and graduate degrees from the University of Southern California. She passed away just two years before I discovered my family tree.

There were only three generations between James William Ayers and me.

One hundred fifty-five years ago, my father's father's father's father was owned by another human being.

Learning these parts of my history meant that, for the first time in my life, I was directly connected to my Black ancestors. I felt vindicated, if only from my own internal struggle, in my nods with other Black people at high school concerts and after President Obama's election, and my frustration with my friends' attempts to set me up.

I felt justified in my frustration with—and guilty for dismissing—the countless instances of white people touching my hair, asking why I don't play sports, and calling me "brotha." Now I felt less white than ever. And for the first time in my life, I could claim my Black side without self-doubt, without hesitation.

DAYS AFTER RECEIVING MY RESULTS, I still wondered about my "66 percent European" DNA. There was no way that could have come completely from my mom's side of the family. I began to wonder whether the man who had enslaved my family, Dr. Ayers (no first name given), and I were connected—maybe even related.

While I had run into constant dead ends researching my ancestors, it was relatively easy to find information about a Dr. Ayers. The Ayers Family Tree says that he owned a plantation in Ashland, Mississippi, which had a population of only one hundred seventy-four people in the 1880 census.

I turned to an 1891 book—which I easily found online— *Biographical and Historical Memories of Mississippi*. There, I learned that a Dr. Augustus Machen Ayres (the spelling has changed over generations) was born in 1821 and buried in Ashland Cemetery in 1890. There was no guarantee that this was the man I was looking for, but he was a doctor, with the correct last name, the right age, in a town of fewer than two hundred people—a very possible match.

I stayed up late one night, digging more into Augustus's story, and I came across a woman who shared our last name and appeared to be a living descendant of his: Karen Ayers Weir. I felt an urgent need to contact her, not for revenge or reparations, but for knowledge—a deeper explanation of who I am and how I got here.

I rattled off an email to Karen in which I introduced myself and briefly summarized my recent discoveries and developments. My email ended with:

> I hold no ill will and I am not after anything at all. That was a different time and our family has since prospered. I am a happy, successful homeowner in Brooklyn, NY with a great job. I am simply fascinated by this process and I want to learn more about the people related to my family—even if they were our owners.

I woke up the next morning to her response.

> Well hello there Nabil!
> I welcome your letter.

Karen surprised me with her excitement and candor—neither of which I was expecting from the woman I'd just gently accused of being the descendant of the man who owned my ancestors.

So in the little bit of information you shared with me, I am
intrigued.

I have worked for a number of years, 26 in fact, on my
genealogy. It has been a passion and at times an obsession.

Some of my Ayers ancestors enslaved people. I am aware
of this, but know that at least some were included as family and
are buried with my ancestors. I hope that was the case always.

I created an image of Karen in my mind. She was older, but
not *old*, possibly in her sixties, with short, cropped, graying
brown hair. I imagined her seated at a kitchen table as she typed
in a modest, cozy home somewhere in the South.

I just looked you up on Facebook and found you! You have
olive-like complexion and look part white. I don't mean anything
negative. Just my observation. Some enslaved people assumed
or took their owners name (don't like this) but for the sake of my
attempt to explain . . . So let's say this Dr. Ayers perhaps was
white and he had a child with one of the enslaved people?

Karen, it turned out, lived in Texas with her husband of forty-
four years. They had several grandchildren. She loved the outdoors
and sent me photos she'd taken of birds and ships on a recent
coastal trip. She had piles of genealogical documents, some of which
she said might be of interest to me. Over days and weeks, our correspondence continued, and we quickly established a rapport:

Hello yourself. Yesterday was a very busy day. We ran about
town all day and were completely worn out. We made healthy
homemade pizza. My half always has black olives, red onion,

feta and mushrooms - my husband's side is less veggies and
more meat. Thin crust. We watched a movie and that was the
entire day.

   The rest of the week is going to be crazy. I did take time to
find the general area of what are sure to be my packed boxes
of genealogy . . .

I began to feel as if Karen and I were living in parallel uni-
verses. Whether or not we shared a bloodline, our ancestors had
lived together in a tiny town, leading very different but very connected lives. And in the strange way of the world, Karen became someone who could fill in some gaps in my history that
had been left open in my father's absence. She had more of my
father's family's history in taped-up boxes than I had gotten in
my entire life.

   Still, I wondered if our different circumstances might be too
much to bridge. She was the descendant of enslavers, and I, the descendant of enslaved people. A small bitterness inside me wanted
Karen to make a wrong move—to expose herself as a racist or a
Confederate. To allow me to feel some anger or resentment for
what her family had done to mine.

   So, after a couple of weeks, I sent Karen the essays I'd published in *The Root* and *HuffPost* about my racial identity and
discovering the strange and powerful Ku Klux Klan history in
Dallas. I was testing the waters. We were fine discussing pizza
and ancient family history, but what if I introduced the subject
of racial injustice within our lifetime?

   The woman was unflappable.

Wow the article about the state fair and the klan was
astounding-

Amazing. I shared it with one of our sons who thought the
same. Thanks.

And so our unorthodox friendship continued.

My father's unavailability had allowed Karen to emerge as
the person with whom to forge a relationship. She was present
and emailing daily. She was interested and helpful—a newfound
resource who could tell me more about my family. There was
no downside to be wary of. No outcome could have been worse
than our real-life scenario as a starting point. It could only go up
from there, as Karen became a window into a much wider part
of my history that even my father might not know.

I became so friendly with Karen that she was the first person
I told about my plan to propose to my girlfriend. I'd just bought
the ring, and even before telling my mother or any close friends,
I emailed a woman I'd never met in person who lived eighteen
hundred miles away.

After several weeks, I realized that I'd told Karen a lot about
myself but hadn't learned much about her beyond her current
life and her ancestors. So I asked her. Her reply was extra-
ordinary.

I was born in Ft Knox Kentucky at a United States Army
Hospital. My father met my mom in Berlin while she was
attending business school. My dad was in Germany for a
couple of years. I have a photo of my mom on the ship
coming to America for the first time. Pretty powerful.

Karen went on to tell me that her grandfather had been a POW in both World War I and World War II, and that he was beaten to near death and imprisoned for stealing potatoes. Then she told me about her mother:

> My mother was forced to be a part of Hitler's youth. She wore a uniform. Hitler abolished all religious activities in Germany, and enticed children and if they didn't adapt to his belief and ideals, it was that or a threat to murder one's families.

For the brief entirety of our relationship, I'd assumed that my ancestors—the ones that Karen's ancestors may have owned—were the only people who struggled. But the story of her grandfather being a POW in two different wars was harrowing. Then I thought about my Black Jewish lineage. What does it mean for me to be corresponding with a woman who was descended from enslavers on her father's side and Nazis on her mother's?

My frequent correspondence with Karen continued, and she started to send bits of genealogical information—letters from the Ayers Farm, photographs of gravestones, family trees that dated back to the 1500s. Even if we weren't related, I was learning more about my ancestry, and Karen and I had fostered an obvious connection.

IN NOVEMBER 2018, I published an essay on *Code Switch*—NPR's race and culture vertical—about my own racial identity and my recent discovery of my family tree. My essay had originally focused on Karen and the possibility that we might actually be related, but my editor pushed me to focus the story on my relationship (or lack thereof) with my father. The final piece was more about what I was missing than about what I'd found—less about my unusual relationship with Karen and more about what it means to have a father who lives in the same city but with whom I have no connection.

When NPR tweeted my story to its seven million followers, I received a mountain of feedback, most of which ended with "I can't wait to see what happens next." That, compounded with the email that Karen sent immediately after she read my story, encouraged me to continue my search. Karen's email read:

> I want you to know I want us to be related. If we are not I think I might feel a measure of disappointment. This isn't over yet. So let me ask you. What you sent today isn't everything is it? Gosh I am hoping there's more.

Karen and I had exchanged dozens of emails and we'd created an obvious connection, but this was the first time she'd expressed a desire for us to be related. Just the thought that she hoped for that—and the fact that she'd opened up the possibility in her mind for the first time—caused me to feel a familial bond.

34.

A Dream about My Father

I was engaged to be married on December 20, 2018, in Los Angeles, where my fiancée AJ grew up and her family still lives. She and I were planning the wedding ourselves, and every detail—from flowers to the seating arrangement—was causing us both to have stress dreams as the event drew closer.

Though I'd never seriously considered inviting Roy to the wedding, I had thought about it. AJ had asked me about it too. I decided not to invite him for one reason: I didn't want my invitation to go unanswered, to float away into the ether, with my wondering if he ever saw it. If I'd thought that my father would have replied—even to say he wouldn't attend—I would have invited him. But I knew how his lack of response made me feel, and his track record for communication had been so poor, I didn't want anything negative to touch our wedding.

I still thought about him, especially in the months leading up to December. I imagined running into him the week of the wedding at the airport or a restaurant. And for the first time, I'd be armed with words. Rather than flustering my way through suggested meetups in New York or small talk about Los Angeles, I would simply say, "I'm getting married on Thursday. Do you want to come?"

Six weeks before the wedding, we selected our photo and gathered some information about ourselves to submit to *The New York Times*, in hopes of appearing in the newspaper's celebrated Vows column. AJ—a writer and editor—did a fantastic job detailing how we met and framing us both as interesting, unique people. The more difficult part was filling out the cold informational form.

Prompts like *education*, *occupation*, *social handle*, and even the ambiguous *noteworthy* box felt easy to answer. But below our own information was a series of questions and answer boxes that required information about our parents. When I thought about my father potentially listed as such, I began to feel uneasy. He didn't raise me and he definitely wouldn't be at the wedding. If our wedding were to be included, would my father receive undeserved credit and praise?

"Relax. It's only information," AJ assured me.

Next to my father's name was an option that solved every problem. "I am not in communication with this parent" was the most satisfying box I'd ever filled in. With one mouse click, we'd relegated my father to a tick in a box, a piece of information with no further connection, emotional or otherwise.

While I'd been able to separate him from the submission form, he was still on my mind, and that night I had a dream—not about our wedding, but about my father.

My dream took place in present-day New York City. In it, Alan and I were at a venue on the city's mature and affluent Upper West Side, tucked into a busy block jammed with colorful bodegas, dry cleaners, and delis. Alan was performing that night, and we were deciding the order in which the other artists would perform at the concert. Just before the show was about to start, I decided to invite my father. He lived nearby, and even though I didn't expect to hear from him, I invited him via text.

In my dream, he replied immediately, saying he'd be right there, that he wants to play with me and Alan.

I've never felt more excited than I felt in that moment.

Maybe music is our form of communication, I thought—a way in which, perhaps, my father is more comfortable, maybe even *most* comfortable. Rather than discovering connections via words, we can do so through music.

It felt like the completion of a cycle: I've played with Alan since I was a child and, before that, Alan had played with my father. Now the three of us would all play together, a family—in some sense—doing what we know best.

As the audience began to gather, I walked by an intellectual couple with glasses and whitening hair. The man stopped talking, and I felt his eyes stick to me as I passed. When he thought I was out of earshot, he said to his wife with great astonishment, "He looks exactly like his father!"

Suddenly, the lights were down and Alan and I were standing onstage before a packed room full of excited people, awaiting our family performance.

A big set of unmanned vibes stood between me and Alan.

And then I woke up.

I have drumming and musical dreams all the time, and it would have been fun to see if we all played together—and *how* we played together. But I'm glad the dream didn't end with the disappointment of my father not showing up.

It ended with the hope that he still might.

35.

And the Grammy Goes to . . .

Toward the end of 2018, as my wedding approached, so did another milestone: my ten-year anniversary at 4AD.

When we released the National's 2013 album *Trouble Will Find Me*, the band was bigger than ever, and for the first time, they were invited to perform on *Saturday Night Live*, a rare, coveted spot for any artist. When our publicist called me with the *SNL* news, I once again felt the personal satisfaction of being in a band. I hadn't written or played the songs, or put in the years of touring and hard work that the National had, but I experienced the fulfillment of being involved. *Trouble* was even nominated for the Best Alternative Music Album Grammy in 2014, but Vampire Weekend—who were signed to XL Recordings, also a Beggars label—won the award.

. . .

WHILE NO ARTIST ON 4AD had yet won a Grammy, we did win another award. Every June in New York, a large contingent from my office attends the A2IM Libera Awards, or the Libbys. The seated dinner and awards ceremony highlight artists and albums on independent record labels. It's grown larger each year, and though artists don't usually attend, hundreds of industry executives vie for the twenty or so awards, like Album of the Year, Marketing Genius, and Label of the Year. Despite the fact that we feel we deserve *every* award each year, 4AD had yet to win a single Libby in the years that led up to the 2016 ceremony.

We'd had great success with Grimes, who was now a superstar who played huge festival stages and graced the covers of major magazines. Grimes was also a video star who not only directed her own videos but did everything from editing to color correcting. That evening, when the emcee announced the fan vote award for Video of the Year, I knew Grimes would win.

Ted Leo, the indie rock royalty host, shouted, "And the winner is . . . Grimes for 'Kill V. Maim!'" I bounced up from our table—fueled by applause—and onto the brightly lit stage, where someone handed me a heavy award statue. The applause died down and I gave a brief, ad-libbed speech that credited Grimes for her amazing work.

Backstage I waited to have my picture taken in line behind two men who had just accepted a Hip-Hop/Rap award. When I congratulated them and introduced myself, one of them replied, "We're huge fans of your work!" I found his compliment strange.

They couldn't have thought that I was Grimes. *I guess they're just big 4AD fans*, I thought. Then the other man chimed in. "Yeah, man, we love all your videos," he said with a smile, mistaking me for the famous video director with whom I share my name.

"No, not that Nabil."

IN JANUARY OF 2018, I returned to the Grammys when the National were again nominated for Best Alternative Music Album for their 2017 album *Sleep Well Beast*. This time they were up against a competitive field that included Arcade Fire and LCD Soundsystem, who were both signed to Columbia Records—a major label that many of us felt had more sway with the voting body. When the award was announced, I sat nervously in my seat among several colleagues, all of whom wanted badly to win but thought the competition was too stiff.

"And the Grammy goes to . . ." a nondescript voice spoke with feigned enthusiasm. "*Sleep Well Beast!*" My colleagues and I shot to our feet, and we made enough noise that everyone in the rows in front of us turned around, expecting to see the band. Only one member of the National, bassist Scott Devendorf, was in town, and he accepted the award by himself. In his sweet, brief speech, Scott thanked his bandmates and then thanked 4AD, mentioning me, my boss Simon, and Beggars Group owner Martin Mills by name. We are not the people who get thanked and we are not the people who need to get thanked, but in that moment, it felt remarkable and it reminded me of how great it was to work at such an artist-friendly record company, how involved I was in the process, and how I didn't actually need to be in a band to feel those feelings.

OVER A YEAR LATER, I'd have the privilege of presenting a platinum album award to Pixies for more than one million American sales of their album *Doolittle*, which was released by 4AD in 1989. And the best part was that it happened backstage at Madison Square Garden immediately following their set. To think that thirty years earlier, I was a seventeen-year-old driving around Salt Lake City in my mom's Toyota, blasting "Monkey Gone to Heaven." And now I was backstage at Madison Square Garden, the place my mother took me to see Kiss—the first band to truly blow my mind—when I was seven. I worried that the band might not share my excitement, but once I presented the award, they couldn't have been happier.

Joey Santiago, Pixies' smiling guitarist, summed it up best as we shook hands for the camera: "The best ones take time."

36.

Los Angeles

On December 20, 2018, AJ and I were married in the Masonic Lodge in the Hollywood Forever Cemetery, in which scores of celebrities are buried. Although some guests found the cemetery to be a strange venue, we really just loved the lodge, which was built in 1931 and emits the understated glow of a century of Hollywood glamour.

We'd asked the DJ to play our entrance music loud—AJ and I were both aware of how powerful and emotional loud music can be. Once our rabbi was onstage, the dramatic violin music from *Fiddler on the Roof*—her entrance music—faded out.

The lights were dim, and as someone pushed open a door, I entered a room of 120 family and friends who all cheered really loud, as if an APPLAUSE sign had lit up. I hadn't anticipated that my own industry trick—dim lighting and loud music—would affect not just the guests but me too. As my mother and her husband, Jim, walked me down the aisle to "Everybody Loves the Sunshine," a wave of emotion swept over me. Most of it stemmed from the wedding and feeling surrounded by my future wife, AJ, family, and friends. But part of it came from the song. My confidence, my unstoppable smile . . . all of this told me that my father was somehow in the room.

AJ walked down the aisle with her mother and her father to the dark synths and thunderous drums of "Atmosphere" by Joy Division, an otherwise brooding song turned euphorically uplifting and beautiful. AJ looked positively radiant as she smiled—with one parent on each arm—and walked slowly toward the stage. Her white designer dress flowed behind her with graceful, symmetrical perfection.

I helped AJ up the stairs, and what followed was our respectful twist on a traditional Jewish wedding. Our rabbi was a woman. We wrote our own vows and AJ led as we said them for the first time in front of our guests. We each had to pause a few times, like when people chuckled over lines I hadn't realized would be considered funny, or when they said "Awww" over sentimental passages, or when I heard one guest in the front row quietly explain to the person next to him what tahini was—the crushed sesame seed paste that is so important in our relationship it made it into our vows.

Then, like that, we were married. I stomped on a glass, and we strutted off the stage to a much more common wedding song, "Crazy in Love" by Beyoncé. We ate, drank, toasted, and danced with our guests, and we experienced the true panic of nearly crashing to the floor as several friends held us high up in the air as we bounced on chairs to the increasing tempo of "Hava Nagila."

AFTER A WHIRLWIND holiday honeymoon in Japan, I found myself back at work in my regular routine. Our wedding already felt like a distant memory until it was prominently featured in *The New York Times*, where it was recounted in great detail. The *Times* piece mentioned my father with a qualifier, "with whom he has had a distant relationship." Reading that line reinstated my need to contact my father, whom I hadn't tried to reach in a couple of years. Like I had in Seattle, I told myself that if I didn't call him now, I might never have the chance again.

The first ring made me anxious, but I reminded myself that it was unlikely a seventy-eight-year-old would pick up the phone after just one ring. The second and third rings brought hope. They took a very long time to pass, during which I felt there was a decent chance I would hear the click of a pickup. The fourth ring was disappointing—the sound of someone either ignoring my call or being unavailable. I assumed the former.

"You have reached . . ." a mechanical female voice over-enunciated. Then my father's voice interjected, speaking his own name. He hadn't answered, but at least I knew the number I had was still his.

I left an upbeat, casual message suggesting that we meet for lunch or coffee. It was a message I would have left for a colleague with whom I might discover common business interests: devoid of emotion, intensity, or motive.

When I hung up, my body responded with an all-too-familiar physical reaction to the realization I'd just made myself vulnerable again. Hope darkened to disappointment, a fast-moving storm invading my body. I could have kicked myself for flippantly taking such a risk. And for what? I hadn't properly thought things through, and now, after the fact, I questioned my own motives. All over again I struggled with one big question:

What do I want from my father?

THE NEXT DAY, Karen Ayers Weir emailed me a photograph of a woman with captivating large brown eyes below a bob of straight black hair and a restrained smile of perfect, white teeth. Her email included only three words: "Your Aunt Royena."

I'd always known the names of my father's three sisters, Thomasina, Royena, and Michelé. I knew them in that order, as if from a line of poetry. I hadn't heard them in the form of a wonderful legend about my father, but rather in the context of one of the few things my mother knew about him. I believed them all to be deceased. Seeing a photograph of my father's sister, my aunt, in her youth made me wish I'd had the chance to meet her. I regretted not having tried years earlier. Karen confirmed that she had indeed passed away in 2015 at the age of seventy-eight.

My mother and Jim had retired to Brooklyn, and that weekend, we had lunch at their apartment in Park Slope. Over spicy chickpea stew, our discussion turned, as it often did, to family, and my mother shared updates on who'd just passed away at ninety-one and who would be joining us for an upcoming "cousins dinner."

When I left, my phone notified me of a new Instagram follower whose profile displayed a recent picture of him with my father above the text "It's always a pleasure to see my uncle Roy and his band perform." It was Karlon, a cousin who looked to be in his twenties and who'd discovered me after randomly reading my NPR essay and realizing we were related. My aunt Royena, whose photograph I'd just received from Karen, was Karlon's grandmother. I direct messaged him and we exchanged phone numbers, promising to speak soon.

I was filled with excitement, and as I walked through Park Slope's tree-lined streets of brownstone homes, I absorbed the sunshine of an unusually nice February afternoon. Feeling bold with the confidence of family members who *did* want to connect, I dialed my father again, hoping that dropping Karlon's name—the name of a family member—might make him more likely to return my call. I left another voicemail, citing the coincidental timing of Karlon's message.

I'd planned on doing some writing in a café that afternoon, and when I opened my laptop, I remembered that in his Instagram message Karlon had also said his mother—my first cousin Rory—had tried to contact me via Facebook but hadn't heard from me. That was strange, I thought, as I regularly check my Facebook messages. But what I'd never noticed was the tab for message requests—messages from people with whom I'm not Facebook friends. As I sat in the café, I found all the messages I'd missed, including one from Rory.

> Good afternoon Cousin! Just read your article in NPR. I'm Rory. We have the same Aunt, Thomasina. Please call me. Let's talk. Very excited!!!

Thankfully, it had been only two days since Rory messaged me. Similar to the way I felt with her son Karlon, the feeling of close family who wanted to connect with me was almost overpowering. After so many years of indifference from my father and then several years of rejection, this felt amazing.

But there were older messages I'd missed too.

One came from a cousin on my mother's side in reference to a piece I wrote for *The New York Times* in 2018 about reissuing Alan's album *Valley of Search*.

> Hi Nabil! I really enjoyed your article in the NY Times. I'm writing to you because I have such a strong memory of meeting you when you were a toddler. I think your grandfather was my grandmother's brother (My grandmother's maiden name was Braufman). This visit was the early '70s, in Boston. I remember you as the most musical toddler I'd ever seen! I remember you banging on everything. I seem to remember your mother brought interesting percussion instruments to the house for you to play. Btw, your uncle looks exactly like another cousin of ours—my sister and I can't get over the resemblance. Small world!

Thanks to her message, she and her sisters later reconnected with my mother, whom they hadn't seen in four decades. When they're all together now, it feels like they're sisters who've known each other since birth.

The final message came from someone from the Baha'i community. It had been sitting in my inbox since 2018.

My Wife Sarah just came across the Valley of Search album article in the NYT. I thought you might enjoy these photos from our wedding at the Cambridge Boat House from 1973. I think Alan is wearing the same shirt in the article photos! We knew Alan and your mom both from the Boston and Amherst Baha'i Community.

Below his message were five black-and-white photos that caused me to well up. Two of the photos are of Alan playing saxophone with a drummer and a bassist. Afros, curls, sideburns, patterns of plaid, and even the way the musicians stand all date stamped the photos 1973. There was also a photograph of me watching two kids play. Another of Alan holding me above his shoulders—I'm not quite two years old. Alan's young eyes convey so much joy, and my smile couldn't be bigger—I'm in the happiest place in the whole world.

The final photo was of Alan and my mother, who is the subject of many, many great photos from every decade. This one stood out to me. It captured their bond and their innocence. She was twenty-three and he was twenty-one. They were raising me with no money and no help. I've never seen a picture in which either of them looks more safe and happy. Alan's thick, young hair, eyebrows, and mustache pull me into his gaze. His arm is around my mother's back, and she looks off camera. Her mouth is open as if she's involved in a conversation, but she knows her picture is being taken. Her flower-print skirt clashes a bit with her XO-pattern blouse, which hangs over a black leotard, but in this moment it looks cool and beautiful.

THAT EVENING I WAS SURPRISED by a call from my new cousin Rory's family, who all shouted "Hello!" at the same time into the speakerphone, as if throwing me a surprise party. Our conversation was light, as if we'd known each other forever. Rory led the call and was joined by her son Karlon and daughter Ryan, and in thirty minutes, I received more information about my family than I had in my entire forty-seven years of life. Rory's mother is Roy's sister Royena, my aunt. And so Rory and I have the same grandparents, Roy I and Ruby. When I mentioned my decade-long attempt to reach my father and Ayana, everyone groaned, as if to say, *That's just how it is.*

Rory was sixty and she spoke with the energy of someone much younger as she matter-of-factly shared information about my family. She and her family knew my father well, and they always saw him when he came to LA, where they lived. When I asked if they'd seen the family tree I'd written about, Rory shouted, "Yeah, do you need it?" The document that had recently changed my life had been sitting with these people, easily available, for all this time. Rory explained that she'd seen my NPR essay by chance and hadn't realized we were related until she showed it to her husband, who said, "You know this is about you, right?"

We made plans to meet in Los Angeles in a couple of weeks. And almost as an afterthought, they mentioned that I should call my aunt Michelé. "We just told her about you, and she'd love to talk to you. She had no idea you existed!" I'd thought that all three of my father's sisters had passed away, but suddenly I was staring at the scribbled phone number of the one who was alive—his youngest sister. And she wanted to talk to me.

I finished the call, then took a deep breath, chugged a glass of water, and dialed my aunt Michelé.

"My nephew. Hi, how are you? I just heard about you. I don't know you, Nabil. How do you pronounce your name?"

Michelé had already pronounced my name perfectly amid her blizzard of excited words. Her tone was warm and comforting, and any apprehension I'd felt immediately disappeared. I explained that I'd known her name for a long time, and she told me that she was the baby, the youngest child, and the only girl living now, and that she missed her older sisters terribly. I had difficulty getting a word in, but I contained myself, feeling more pleased with Michelé's excitement than I would from speaking or asking questions. It was powerful to hear such welcoming words from my father's sister.

When asked, I explained how I came to exist: my twenty-one-year-old mother had been kind of dating my father—Michelé's brother—and told him she wanted a child. He agreed, with the caveat that he wouldn't be involved.

"And here I am," I concluded.

"He never told us. He never told *me*." Michelé sounded not angry, but greatly surprised and disappointed in her older brother, whom she obviously admired. "I just can't believe that he would not claim you, and it sounds like he denied you."

This woman—my aunt, my father's sister who'd known my father for her entire seventy-six years of life—had no idea I existed.

ONE WEEK LATER, I flew to Los Angeles for a last-minute work meeting. The only nonwork call I made was to my aunt Michelé so we could meet in person for the first time.

Over a two-hour lunch, I learned that my aunt is a sweet, caring, lovable woman with a sharp, snappy wit. We share the same high cheekbones and full smile. The funny thing was, we also both wear oversized, black, thick-framed glasses, which are kind of my trademark. She talks a lot, but when she doesn't, she exudes silent power. She could easily pass for my mother.

Michelé possesses a physicality that reminded me of my few brief but affecting interactions with my father, whom she described in the same way my mother and I always have: charismatic. "He was always all about that music!" Michelé punctuated her compliment about my father's charisma with a story about his early obsession with music that she seemed almost annoyed to tell. She told me he saw the vibraphonist Lionel Hampton at a young age and immediately knew that's what he wanted to do—who he wanted to be. I nodded slowly, contemplating the way my aunt described my father—it was exactly the same way my mother describes me. Through a connectedness that transcended our distance, I'd followed more closely in my father's footsteps than I'd ever known.

I spent the first hour of our lunch learning about my aunt and her childhood, which, she told me repeatedly, was wonderful. She was born in their family's home in Los Angeles, the youngest of four children, two years after my father. Her parents, Roy I and Ruby, were from Oklahoma, children of successful farmers. She thought that her mother, my grandmother, had grown up wealthy because she'd had her own horse and buggy when she was in high school. Both of Ruby's brothers had become doctors and moved to Los Angeles, where the rest of the family eventually joined them.

"We were raised *right*." Michelé carried some of the eccentricities of a cool aunt, but just when she started to go down that route, she'd return with a snappy, proper statement. "Churchgoing. God-fearing." She spoke those words slowly and deliberately.

"So let me ask you this. Does he own you?" Michelé maintained eye contact while I processed her question: she wanted to know whether my father acknowledged that I was his son.

I explained that we'd met several times, briefly, during my childhood. And that in our last meeting over a decade ago, he did *own* me to the extent that he never questioned that he was my father.

"If my mother knew that she had another grandchild, believe me, you would know her. She was just a wonderful, *wonderful* woman, and she really cared about her grandchildren."

My heart warmed when my aunt mentioned my paternal grandmother. Then she opened a heavy bag containing several pictures in decorative frames. I thought about how much work it must have taken to pack them up, and I assumed she'd done so

on her own—her husband Zelber had passed away a few years
ago. In the restaurant crowded with elderly folks who spoke loud
and waiters who spoke louder, the photos covering the lace ta-
blecloth in front of me made all the noise disappear.

The most powerful image was of my grandparents when they
were in their twenties, newlyweds who looked innocent but self-
assured, my grandfather in a sharp pinstriped suit and my grandmother in a wool coat over a white blouse. My grandmother's
image offered further validation—her brown eyes looked just
like mine.

Michelé, her sisters, and my father had grown up in a large
house with a piano; their father owned the service station next
door. She described their neighborhood as Black, with a few
Hispanic families, but every time I tried to talk about race, Michelé acted as if there were nothing to discuss. She'd grown up in
a happy, safe place. As much as I wanted my aunt to tell me that
she'd been a Black Panther, I was more than relieved to hear that
she'd spent her life living her life. She hadn't had to fight for
what she had. After I took shoddy iPhone pictures of her family
photographs, I helped place the bag of photos in the back seat of
her newish black Mercedes when the valet pulled it around.

As I walked to my car, I studied the photo I loved the most. It
was of the entire family: my father, his three sisters, and their
parents. My father looked to be about eight, so it was likely taken
around 1948. Everyone was wearing their Sunday best. Pressed
suits, long dresses, and corsages told me that the family was at

least moderately well off. Only my father and Michelé—the two youngest—looked happy to be getting their picture taken. Everyone else held impatient looks, and all of their hands told a story. My grandfather's left hand draped lazily over his right. Royena appeared to be anxiously playing with her ring. My grandmother Ruby, Thomasina, and Michelé each clasped their fingers formally, as if they could remain seated for hours if necessary. And Roy's hands were strangely twisted with his thumbs interlocked. His was the biggest smile, like he was ready to scamper out of the room the moment the flash started to fade.

I wanted to walk into this room. I wanted to know what it smelled like and whether the ceilings were high enough for my voice to trail off like it did in a big house. What did the carpet feel like, and did it dull the sound of the piano my father played? What books were on the shelves?

I wondered what each of the six personalities in the photograph was like. Thomasina, the oldest, looked the least happy to be there, and I equated her, based on her facial expression, with the photos I'd seen of my half sister Ayana. My grandfather looked a lot like Mtume and also like Eboni—the three of them had similar noses.

I wanted to know my grandparents now, and I wanted to know them as a child, the way I knew my maternal grandparents. I wanted to ride shotgun in a car that was loud and imposing while my grandfather drove. I wanted to hear my grandmother tell me stories about her parents and her grandparents. And to tell me which of them I reminded her of most. I wanted to meet them at the age they were in the photo, likely in their forties. And

I wanted to meet my father and his sisters at the age they were in the photo. Meeting my father as an eight-year-old might have better explained who he was than meeting him when he was older. Eight-year-olds are honest, carefree, and without motive. They want to play, to eat, and to speak their minds. I wanted to meet my father under those conditions more than I wanted to meet him now, when he was a protective, self-involved adult.

As I scrolled through the photographs, I thought about the cosmic timing that had been at work in the background: Roy may have not answered my call one week ago, but after I left my voicemail, I received a wave of information from Karen, Karlon, and some Baha'is I hadn't seen in decades. And now I was speaking with my cousins and dining with my aunt. When I considered how I'd arrived at this moment, I suddenly felt awestruck: the two essays I'd published about family had directly connected me to *new* family. I was doing the work of researching and contacting people, and the chronicling and publishing of that work had turned out to be the most connective and rewarding part of the process.

37.

West Coast Vibes

Two weeks after my lunch with my aunt Michelé, I was back in Los Angeles again, where I was greeted by three smiles that looked like mine. Michelé and my cousins Karlon and Ryan were at a table in the back of a spacious Mexican restaurant with strong tables, clay tile floors, and colorful paintings on the walls.

Rory's kids, Karlon and Ryan, both stood up for hugs at our first in-person meeting. Karlon was nearly seven feet tall, lanky but athletic, with a kind, soft demeanor. Ryan carried the same calm strength and wore glasses under a hip black hat. They both said my name correctly—something I never expect from anyone, even family. Karlon was twenty-seven and working on his master's degree in public health. Ryan was twenty-five and finishing her master's degree in social entrepreneurship. He ran track and she modeled, neither of which surprised me one bit.

Though we'd recently met, Michelé looked different from our first meeting. Then, she wore thick-framed black glasses. Today, she wore a pair of red glasses and her hair was out, demonstrating what she'd told me last time: "I have fabulous hair." As I leaned down to hug her, I was careful to make sure our big glasses didn't bump.

She gave me a hard kiss on the cheek and said "Hi, honey," reminding me in the most comforting, accepting way of my maternal grandmother Jean.

Soon Rory and her husband "Big Karlon" arrived with more hugs. Both were comfortably dressed down for the weekend, Rory in a yellow sweatshirt over a black turtleneck and Big Karlon in a cozy wool jacket. We talked about the weather for a minute—it was unusually cold in LA.

When small talk subsided, Michelé asked Rory what she was doing. But Rory had lost the conversation—she was staring at me, smiling.

"I'm looking at family," Rory responded calmly. Thus began an hour-long conversation that, despite six of us at the table, was predominantly between me and Rory. At sixty, she was old enough to know things: our shared grandparents, the house in LA where everyone had grown up, family stories . . . she'd been around for lots of it. Yet she was young enough to maintain her strong memories and recount them with accuracy. She knew my father well. She emerged as the holder of the most information—with which she was quite generous.

I continually made the mistake of thinking these people knew my story, possibly because I felt as comfortable around them as I did with all good friends and family. So I was taken aback when they asked the most basic questions—like if I ever saw my father.

"I saw him last week," Michelé piped up proudly. "I sat on the side of the stage and he was *wonderful!*" She made the boasting face of a young girl describing her pet pony: as if it were something only she had and nobody else.

Karlon interjected with a story of a recent trip to London during which he'd discovered "Uncle Roy" was performing. He got there but the show was sold out and the bouncer didn't believe that he was a relative. I thought about what I would have done in his situation: I'd have said to the bouncer, "Look at me." The hard part for me wouldn't have been getting in, it would have been deciding to even try in the first place. But I didn't say that out loud.

I briefly retold the story of me and my father to a table full of concerned faces. Then I retracted and balanced out the sadness to talk about my mother. She'd had me deliberately and planned on raising me on her own. It had always been her and me, with help from my uncle, and she did an amazing job.

"Yes, she did," Rory replied with a serious look. All heads nodded in agreement. Then Rory chimed in with the hard questions.

"So do you identify as Black?" The table silently awaited my answer.

I explained that I wasn't sure, and I worried about offending the five family members who surrounded me, people who I knew did identify as Black. I'd now seen their family photos, which showed years and generations of Black partners, husbands, and wives.

"But I don't identify as white," I added. And I returned to the story of my childhood, in which it wasn't necessary for anyone to belong to any race.

"He's just him!" Michelé interrupted with a stern look, as if telling Rory to back off. But I didn't feel attacked—rather, I felt engaged in a topic I love exploring.

The question "How did you feel growing up?" hit me in the gut. Though I wanted to be asked those questions, I didn't necessarily want to answer them. I just wanted someone other than my mother to be curious enough to ask . . . to want to know my answers. This, I realized, was what it felt like to have family. I'd been unknowingly craving this type of acceptance for years. Suddenly, my lunch with my father felt a lot more like small talk.

And that's when it hit me. I knew my father didn't doubt that I was his son. I also knew he'd never be a real father. But there was something that existed between those two extremes. The reason I left our lunch twelve years earlier feeling informed but unsatisfied was because my father never asked questions like the ones Rory did. He never asked me how I felt about his agreement to give my mother a child but not be involved, how it felt to grow up without a father, how it felt to lack a strong racial identity, or whether I had any anger toward him or my mother. But now, with Rory's questions stirring inside me, it all became more clear.

Though my mother was the first to admit that she had no idea what she was doing when she gave birth to me, she trusted her instincts and surrounded us with positive, nurturing, and protective people. My fatherless childhood memories felt cherished and celebratory. I didn't need my father's help to understand who I was. As Michelé had sternly stated, I was just me.

When I felt our lunch winding down, I mentioned Eboni. I felt worried doing so—I was barely in the door myself, and though I already felt connected to these people, they had no proof that we were related aside from my NPR essay, my word, and my face. To add another person into the mix right now might be pushing it, like it could cause the miraculous house I'd just carefully built to crumble. But to not mention Eboni felt unfair. She was just as related as I was, and we'd met because of our shared need to uncover family.

I passed around my phone, which displayed a recent picture of me and Eboni smiling in the sun on a Philadelphia park bench. Everyone took a look at the photo, likely looking for a resemblance to themselves. They nodded their heads, but nobody commented, and I didn't push it. It was as if Eboni didn't exist because she wasn't at the table—there was only one open seat that day, and I'd occupied it.

I had more questions on my mind: What about my grandfather's family on the side that Mtume had mentioned at our lunch? What about my DNA results with nearly no Native American blood? But it felt too early to introduce these confrontational topics.

At Rory's insistence, our waiter took a photo of us, and when I texted it to AJ, she replied, "There are three of you!" Indeed, my aunt, my cousins, and I all had the same smile. As I looked at the picture, I felt lucky to be among blood relatives—new family who were just one click away from me. It boggled my mind to think they'd always been there—ready to meet me, ready to share information, to talk and hug.

When Rory mentioned a family reunion, I replied, "It sounds like there are a lot of us."

I'd never felt more nervous tossing out such a simple phrase—one that would not generally seem loaded or at risk of arousing suspicion. But at this moment, when I'd just met my cousins for the first time, the term "us" represented more than the six people at the table. It meant family. But that "us" could also have been dangerously premature.

Rory nodded thoughtfully, explaining that there had been barbecues in the past, and that it might be time for another one. She said so without acknowledging my use of "us," and when I detected no reaction from anyone else at the table, I relaxed, feeling one giant step closer to being included.

As I learned more about my father, I was discovering my family members. The end goal was unclear to me, and that was perhaps the most exciting part of my pursuit. Each door I opened revealed a new one, and though I knew none would open to my father, I was learning more about myself and my family in the process.

38.

Inglewood Park Cemetery

A few months later, in July 2019, I was back in Los Angeles. It was hot on Ventura Boulevard, in the San Fernando Valley just over the Hollywood Hills. I was headed to my aunt Michelé's house. As it stood, I'd arrive six minutes early, which I overthought and decided placed me in one of two categories: anxious or annoying. I didn't want to be perceived as either in the still—I hoped—early stages of my relationship with my aunt. I killed a little time by pulling into the corner gas station for two bottles of water—we'd made plans to visit my grandparents' grave, and I knew we'd be stuck in traffic and outside in the heat a lot today.

As gravity pushed my back against the seat on the steep, twisting drive to Michelé's house, the thoughts that swirled around my brain ranged from the most simple: *What if she forgot about our meeting and isn't home?* To the more complicated: *What if she doesn't recognize me?* To the most anxiety inducing: *What if she thinks I want something—her house, her car?* She lived in a nice neighborhood, and the houses grew more impressive with each turn and each rapid elevation climb.

I arrived at Michelé's driveway and saw her black Mercedes, which told me she was home. I could see the two-story navy blue home with clean white trim and beyond it, across the valley, which appeared to be at a drastically lower elevation below where I stood.

"Hi, baby." My aunt greeted me with a strong hug, and instantly all my cares were gone. "Come in," she prodded me in a gently scolding tone that accused me of being unnecessarily formal by standing outside her open door. Her energy felt as happy and as excited as mine.

Michelé's home was open and bright, full of windows that looked out on the valley. Every room was crowded—but not cluttered—with African American knickknacks: smiling, heavy-set faces with round bodies that served as cookie jars and teakettles; dozens of ceramic watermelon-themed objects; a boisterous Black Santa Claus holding a long cane and standing about four feet tall. Near the front door, a collection of Nutcracker dolls redefined something that felt traditional but now looked different simply based on their brown skin and black hair.

"Thomasina came here once." Michelé spoke of her deceased older sister. "She said, 'There sure are a lot of *Black* things in here.' And I said, 'Ain't no *white* people living here!'"

The staircase to the second floor was a museum dedicated to my family. Photographs of people I now recognized—my father, my aunts, my grandparents—stood out among pictures of others whom I'd never seen. Some photographs were much older, possibly from the 1800s, and I wondered whether or how I was related to the serious-looking subjects. I immediately recognized one picture of my grandmother when she was in her twenties. She wore a fuzzy sweater, and pearls emphasized her neckline. I saw myself in her, but she had a full head of straight, long hair.

Once we were in the car, Michelé started telling stories, and I just listened and smiled as I drove. She and her deceased husband Zelber—whom she simply called Z—once traveled to Egypt. When they landed, she cried, because her father had never flown and it meant a lot to her to be suddenly surrounded by men who looked so much like him. "Daddy?" she wanted to ask some of the men.

As a teenager, Michelé was allowed to go on dates, but she had a midnight curfew. Before her father went to bed, he left an alarm clock in the bathroom set for midnight. If it went off, that meant she hadn't come home in time. "That alarm never once went off. Daddy wasn't strict, he was *right*." She defended her liberal curfew and the fact that at the time, she was going on her first dates with Z.

When Michelé started to talk about my father, she asked again if I'd met him, and I retold my story, ending with his non-response to my recent phone calls. "That's just him," she said. "When he was a teenager, he had a job at a big department store downtown. Everybody *loved* him, but he'd play music at night and show up late and he was always tired at work, so they fired him." This only reinforced her previous stories of my father's dedication to music—his obsession.

We pulled into a California-sized Vons supermarket, and Michelé instructed me to choose three clusters of large, bright sunflowers, "Mommy's favorite." As I picked over a large bushel of sunflowers that all looked the same—perfect—I noticed two women at the counter looking at us and smiling. I assumed that they thought I was her son. We looked alike and the age difference was right. And I thought that it might be the first time in my life that someone had quickly assumed without reservation that someone was my mother.

As we pulled into the cemetery, I saw the Forum, where I'd attended a concert just over a year ago. And I thought how strange it was that I was unknowingly practically across the street from my grandparents' grave that night.

First we visited Zelber's grave, where we stood in the warm early afternoon sun. Michelé spoke to Z about her new nephew and how I was a nice young man. It made me feel connected to Z, and I wished I could have met the man who looked so cool and strong in the many photos I'd now seen. I was touched to hear my aunt say such loving words to the person she spent most of her life with and obviously missed terribly.

After a long walk with our arms linked, Michelé and I stood before the gravestone of her parents—my grandparents. There was just one shared gravestone, a two-foot-wide dark stone plank that, like every grave in this section, was flush with the ground. It wasn't flashy or ostentatious, but it wasn't sad or decrepit either. It was solid, present, and effective—the stone of two people who wanted to be together forever.

AYERS was the first line, in all caps. The name was familiar—I saw it every day—but in this context, it felt less like mine, and my first thought was to wonder whether my grandparents were in the ground thinking, *Is this the guy who* decided *to use* our *name?*

BELOVED FATHER AND MOTHER lay below AYERS. Their names and dates were below that: ROY E. 1905–1969 and RUBY M. 1907–1985. They were close in age, I thought to myself, but Ruby outlived Roy by a long time—sixteen years.

As if at a ceremony, Michelé and I stood naturally, facing the grave, looking down, with our arms still linked. "Hi, Mama." She spoke in a voice similar to the one she used with Z but less as an equal—more with the tone of a daughter than a wife. "This is your grandson Nabil." She spoke slowly, allowing the moment of my introduction to hang a bit longer. It was moments like these—the moments of affirmation—that I cherished the most. Rory staring at me and saying she's looking at family. And now Michelé telling my grandmother that I was her grandson.

"He's a really nice young man and . . . I'm sorry you didn't get to meet him. I think you would really, really like him." For a moment Michelé's conversation with her mother was so good it almost felt forced—as if she were going to break character, turn to me, and say, "Is this what you want? Am I doing it right?" But she didn't, and I could hear the sincerity in her slightly shaky voice. "Okay, I miss you so much and I'll see you soon." I breathed in a big breath and let out a long sigh, awaiting my aunt's words for my grandfather.

But Michelé said, "Okay, ready?" as I felt her arm tug mine.

"What about grandpa?" I asked, in a voice that I immediately thought sounded too accusatory.

Michelé continued to turn away, as if she'd never considered waiting for what I'd just asked for. "Oh, he doesn't care."

Her words hit deep, and I began to laugh as we walked away from the grave. Her words about her father, though simple to her, meant a lot to me. They told me that my grandmother was the caregiver in the family, the emotional supporter, the heart. When I'd met Roy in 2006, he'd told me stories about his supportive mother, but none about his father. That, coupled with what Michelé had just said, helped me to better understand why it might be easy for my father to be so disconnected from me. It was possible that in ignoring me he wasn't doing anything active or deliberate—maybe it was because, like his own father, he just didn't care.

As we walked to the car, I wondered why the men in my family—at least the two before me—were this way. I didn't have children, but I couldn't imagine being able to feel that way. Perhaps my desire—my *need*—to connect came from my mother. The further I delved into this search for information about my family and into myself, the more I realized that in some ways I was the opposite of my father. While he was in the city where I lived, unable to return my calls, I was three thousand miles from home in a cemetery with his sister, being introduced to his dead mother.

I thought about the many family connections that the men in my family had failed to make. Now I was being told that even my dead grandfather wasn't interested in an introduction—a simple hello. Suddenly my position felt more like a role: to break a pattern and to be a male connector in the family. It was a role I was now more positive than ever I'd inherited from my mother.

LUNCH THAT AFTERNOON with Rory, Karlon, and Big Karlon was as comfortable as it had been last time. But when Rory mentioned "Uncle Roy," I tensed up, feeling in the familiar hot seat, the spotlight. I had to remind myself that these people actually knew Roy and they were simply referring to their relative.

We talked about my job but not too much, because my new LA family got it: Rory had worked in the music business before becoming a teacher—some of that time for Roy's production company. It was a relief not to have to explain that no, I wasn't a producer, and yes, record companies still existed.

They mentioned Roy in the same sentence as Marvin Gaye and Stevie Wonder; they mentioned the singer Dee Dee Bridgewater, which felt full circle for me—I knew that Dee Dee sang on albums with both Roy and Alan. At one point, Big Karlon mentioned something about the music of "our people." And when he said "our people," he made eye contact with me in a way that felt inclusive.

I was sitting at a table with close relatives whom I'd met only once before. And already they considered me to be family.

39.

Everybody Loves the Sunshine

In the spring of 2020, as the world struggled through the coronavirus pandemic, another plague came into focus: the lynching of Black people. After the killings of Ahmaud Arbery, Breonna Taylor, George Floyd, and so many others, much of America was fed up, and in its own way, so was the music industry.

One week after George Floyd's death, Brianna Agyemang and Jamila Thomas, two Black women in the New York music industry called for Blackout Tuesday, a day for the music industry to protest by shutting down completely. Rather than simply giving our staff the day off on June 2, 2020, we asked people to use the day constructively—whatever that meant to them. I thought about what that meant to me. I could write—something I typically did with free time, and perhaps I'd dig deeper into my feelings about race. I could read and listen to music by the Black authors and artists whom I loved. But none of that felt special. Then I had an idea.

A few months earlier, I'd reconnected with Ed Eckstine, the Mercury Records president who had helped sign my band the Lemons back in 1995. Although we hadn't spoken since our brief meeting twenty-five years earlier, it felt like time. I had an easy time contacting Ed online, and he agreed to meet me for a meal. That day, when I entered the Los Angeles restaurant where we met for breakfast, I immediately recognized his larger-than-life persona.

I explained to Ed that our short meeting in 1995 had left some questions in my head that didn't feel appropriate to ask at the time, and that during that meeting, I wasn't thinking about my band, I was thinking about my father and the fact that Ed likely knew him, because of his background in the R&B music world.

Ed's response came out as casually as his omelet order. "Yeah," he said, "of course I've crossed paths with Roy."

I spent the next hour absorbing Ed's incredible life story. His father was the big band singer Billy Eckstine, and Ed had landed his first real gig at eighteen as Quincy Jones's right hand in his new record and production company, Qwest. Ed walked me through his own impressive career trajectory, which brought him from one great gig to the next and quickly to the position of president at Mercury Records. He'd been lucky to have his father's music business connections, but he was also smart and talented, and he'd made great decisions. I saw a lot of myself in Ed, and I regretted waiting twenty-five years to reach out to him.

So, when Blackout Tuesday arrived, my meeting with Ed came to mind, and I immediately decided to call him again, one Black music industry executive speaking to another on a day to pause and reflect. Then the entrepreneurial side of my brain kicked in: *What if I turned our conversation into a piece for* The New York Times? First thing Monday morning, I emailed an editor who responded quickly, saying that the *Times* was planning extensive coverage of Blackout Tuesday, and that she'd like our conversation to run as soon as possible within the news cycle.

On Blackout Tuesday, Ed and I spoke on the phone for ninety minutes about issues of race and racism in the music industry. I learned that Ed had been instrumental in signing New Order and that he'd felt some resistance when he took over Mercury Records, whose roster included three massive white rock bands: Bon Jovi, Def Leppard, and Kiss. Ed and I agreed that while it was good that the major labels set up R&B departments and staffed them mostly with Black employees, this also created segregation within the industry in which white people worked on the rock side and Black people on the R&B side. And we discussed the word "urban," a term that had meant something important when it represented the radio stations that catered to large populations of Black city listeners but was now a controversial catchall that simply meant "Black."

The day after my piece ran in *The New York Times*, Universal/Republic—the largest of the major labels—announced that it would immediately drop the term "urban" from its description of music and its departments. The next week the Grammy Awards announced that the word "urban" would be removed from every award title that had previously included it. These discussions were already happening, but clearly I'd found myself in the middle of an exciting sea change, a shift of attitudes. Two major labels then each committed to $100 million funds to benefit Black artists. That, combined with the proliferation of black squares on social media channels in solidarity with the Black Lives Matter movement, felt heartening. Sure, some of the social media posts, donations, and statements from individuals to major corporations seemed like grandstanding, but it was impossible not to notice people's commitment to change, and in my own small way, I was part of it.

IN JULY 2020, AJ AND I were house-sitting in Los Angeles, enjoying the mild weather and extra space now that we were both working from home—but also feeling nomadic and disconnected, like so many people during the pandemic.

One morning I received a text from Eboni. She and I texted on and off and it was always light: happy birthday messages, pictures of her kids, an article I'd written. We rarely spoke, but it was comforting to know that she was there, and to feel the security of someone with whom I had so much in common.

Eboni's text said she needed to talk as soon as possible. It contained no hearts or smiley faces like most previous texts had in our yearslong thread. My first thought was that I'd said or written something to offend her. But I knew I'd done nothing disparaging.

"Are you sitting down?" After a brief catchup and confirmation of everyone's health and safety, Eboni got right to the point, explaining that she'd finally taken a DNA test and that the results named someone else as her father. Her mother had then confirmed that she'd had a brief relationship with the man. So we weren't blood relatives after all.

"I don't care" were the first words that came out of my mouth.

Five years earlier, when I'd met Eboni for the first time, my heart filled with joy and hope—feelings that replaced four decades of mystery and a decade of ambivalent rejection from my father. Eboni's story about sneaking backstage and hoping to meet Roy had resonated with me. My connection with her gave me the confidence to invest more energy and to connect with my new Los Angeles relatives. Without Eboni, I might not have had the courage to drive up the emotionally and physically winding road to Michelé's house to take her on that trip to my grandparents' grave.

As I explained all this to Eboni, I realized how much better it made her feel, how it allowed her to worry less about what I and others close to her might think. She breathed a long sigh of relief, and we agreed that our DNA doesn't always matter.

DNA is only one way to measure family.

I can still hear the young voices of Eboni's sons the first time they smiled and shouted without hesitation, "Hey, Uncle Nabil!" My mother remains close with Eboni's mother Verrona, and every time they speak, my mother updates me in the same proud way she does with her many lifelong cousins. When Eboni told me she would soon meet her real father—a man whose excitement matched her own—I even felt connected to him. And for the first time I felt the deep, personal satisfaction that I'd often heard about from people with siblings.

Eboni was my sister in all the ways that mattered.

IF I'VE LEARNED ANYTHING in my search to connect with my father, it's that family is what you make it. Family is a living, evolving construct. It's what you allow it to be, and if you're lucky, it's what you want it to be. In my case, family is more than I could have ever expected.

Is Roy my family?

Yes, I inherited his almondine eyes and high cheekbones, and when bartenders see my name on my ID, they sometimes ask, "Any relation?" When we had lunch together in Seattle, I was blown away by our laughs and the specific mannerisms that connected us. Sometimes when I watch old performances of his online, I see the playful zip that I feel in my own body. But DNA doesn't always make for family.

What about what he's taught me . . . does that make Roy my family? That's a hard question to answer. I don't think there's anyone else in my life who's given me so much through the very fact of their absence.

Thanks to Roy, I have an unwavering sense of independence. Between a nonexistent father and a mother who was in school or at work full time for my entire childhood, I spent a lot of time on my own. I learned to shop, cook, clean, and take care of myself at a very young age. I learned how to keep my wits about me. How to talk to strangers and how *not* to talk to strangers. How to initiate and finish conversations. How to observe and take in my surroundings. How to participate and how to distance myself. Sometimes my independence exists to a fault—when I feel and act like I don't need anyone. But generally, it's an attribute for which I'm grateful.

I also think I have Roy to thank for my confidence. Unbeknownst to me, the way he carried himself in our brief run-ins, on his album covers, and in photographs all taught me that he thought highly of himself, and that it was okay, even important, to have all eyes turn toward you when you entered a room. I picked up on this early, and it helped me get through my adolescent years, during which I could have stood out as the racially mixed kid without a father. Instead, I stood out as the drummer from New York whom everybody wanted to befriend.

And Roy taught me how to live in the present. When I met him for lunch in Seattle, I was impressed, even baffled, by his ability to connect and to bring everything down to earth, in what could have—should have—been a very uncomfortable situation for him. He chose to *not* make our meeting about apologizing or making up for lost time—two things it was evident he had no interest in doing. He wanted to live in the present and do so in a genuine, engaged, and meaningful way. It's a skill that's useful to a point, but also one that's not always positive. I've tried to improve upon this trait by being in tune with the things my father is unable or unwilling to recognize, creating a world of people whom I love and who love me. Creating a family.

Roy is likely responsible for my musical aptitude. But I can't discount my mother and Alan's contributions either: buying me drums and records, taking me to concerts, and surrounding me with musicians from an early age—constantly and unwaveringly supporting my interest in music in ways that required care and effort. My life in music is a living example of nature versus nurture, and both sides have contributed equally.

Inheritance aside, is Roy my family?

In trying to answer that, I think about the large cast of characters who took over where he left off: Gene Ashton (Cooper-Moore) and the residents of 501 Canal, who seemingly existed for no other reason than to make powerful music and treat people with kindness. The Baha'i communities in Cambridge and Amherst that ingrained in me the importance of diversity, equality, and delicious meals. Diane and Tony, our neighbors who were *so* similar to us that it was impossible to feel other. Dave, the drum teacher who made me a better musician and exposed me to a world of new music. Benny, who got me my first job in New York City. Ron, the Salt Lake City timpanist who paid for my concert tickets when my mother was unemployed. Shannon, who loved and protected me like her own son. And Jim, who took over for me when I went away to college.

And I think about the family I've found. The family I've created.

Now I have Eboni, with whom I exchange texts on birthdays,

graduations, and other celebratory events. I have Karen, who is always there, whether for a casual check-in or an intense piece of ancestral information. The first time she sent me a birthday card, I was choked up by the simple, thoughtful gesture. Now I enjoy the security of knowing that she'll send a birthday card every year. I have an aunt and cousins in Los Angeles. When Rory sent me a simple three-word text, "We miss you!," accompanied by a photo of everyone at the Thanksgiving dinner I was unable to attend, my body filled with warmth. And I can physically feel the proud way Michelé looks at me—like she's been looking at me that way since I was a baby. I have new homes, landmarks, and gravestones to visit. I didn't meet any of these people until I was in my forties—Karen and I have still never met, and we still don't know if we're actually related. But these relationships transcend traditional family because we've allowed them to; we've decided that they matter.

And I have AJ, the love of my life, who has opened a new world of parents, grandparents, a sister, aunts, uncles, and cousins with whom I feel included and grounded.

And I will always, always have my mother and Alan. I think about them in that photo from the wedding in 1973, when we were living day to day, never thinking about what was missing—only about the happy simplicity of our lives. They both made sacrifices in order to improve my life. And they were always honest about Roy, making a steady attempt to expose him to me as much as possible. And if I ever became uncomfortable around him, they allowed me to say, "That's enough."

When I look back on people's reactions to my childhood

stories—as if they thought something was wrong—now more than ever I know that nothing was wrong. When I think about the people who have questioned my mother's choice to have me the way she did, or the people who have asked me if I was ever angry with her, it's easier than ever to answer no, rejecting the antiquated assumption that a real father is a necessary element in a real family.

So is Roy my family?

It's hard to comprehend that my father maintained so much presence in my life, despite only a handful of human interactions. In that sense, he's been ever present—a mythical figure who barely exists in real life, but who always exists through his music. When I think back to that movie theater in 2015—where my father's music made me feel hot, short of breath, and internally full of panic—I'm reminded of everything that's happened since then, everything that's changed, the wealth of people with whom I've been able to connect and call family.

When I hear "Everybody Loves the Sunshine"—which happens more often than ever—the opening chords still catch me off guard. But now the lazy synthesizer melody allows me to relax. I hear and feel it with a new sense of appreciation—a new sense of connection. As my father's voice shoots out from the speakers and into the warm light, I smile and quietly sing along:

"My life, my life, my life, my life . . . in the sunshine."

Acknowledgments

Thank you to my brilliant, beautiful wife, Ally Jane Ayers, for giving me the love and strength to write about the difficult topics. Without you, this book would not exist.

Thank you to my editor, Meg Leder, who helped me bring this book to life by insisting that reality is more powerful than fantasy. And thank you to everyone at Viking/Penguin.

Thank you to my agent, Meg Thompson, whose confidence and guidance made for an incredible book-writing experience.

Thank you to Michael Azerrad, whose early help and encouragement convinced me I could write a book.

Thank you to Louise and Jim Vesper, Alan Michael Braufman and Shannon Michael, Jesse Michael, Will Michael and Mayumi Namikoshi, Jean and Bert Braufman, Joe and Edith Chesler, Peter and Maguy Bronson, Michael and Doris Bronson, Sue and Joe Peragallo, Jason Peragallo and Ciara Curtin, Rob Brofman and Justin

Pertschuk, Diane and Tony Randall, and my many maternal cousins for creating and helping me to recall these memories.

Thank you to Mtume Ayers, Eboni Jackson-Mathis, Joseph and Joshua McLeod, Verrona Gibson, Fountain Bailey Murray, Karen Ayers Weir, Rory and Karlon Johnson, Michelé Minnix, Karlon Johnson Jr., Ryan Johnson, and Estevan Carlos Benson for your willingness to connect, and for your help in connecting me with others.

Thank you to Susan Silverberg, Mark and Shannon Grossan, Madison Grossan, Murray and Rosalyn Grossan, Melissa Grossan and Norm Garland, Bruce Grossan and Mylene Mogendorff, Sheldon and Paula Silverberg, Jonny Silverberg and Jess Jervinsky, and Jolene Frankie Silverberg for welcoming me into the West Coast family.

Thank you to the influencers: Cooper-Moore, Marzette Watts, Tom Bruno, Tom Kyle, Doane Perry, Nabil Sater, Benny Bruno, Ron Holdman, Dave Jette, Jay Kramer.

Thank you to the editors who took a chance on a new writer, believed in my stories, and helped me to improve them: Richard Martin, Sean Nelson, Danielle Belton, Noah Michelson, Bill Ferguson, Sam Hockley-Smith, Leah Donnella, Chris Gayomali, Alanna Okun, Hanif Abdurraqib, Alex Apatoff, Brooke Hauser, Ray Isle, Oset Babür, Caryn Ganz, Jillian Mapes, Jeremy Larson, Anna Gaca, Chloe Sarbib, Simon Vozick-Levinson, Ryan Dombal. And thank you to the subjects of some of those pieces: Dan Reynolds, Ed Eckstine, Frederique Boudouani.

Thank you to the friends who connected me with editors and agents: Carrie Tolles, Kate Jackson Mendel, Ali Hedrick, John Chao, Marcus J. Moore, Nils Bernstein, Brigitte Green, Ann Banks.

Thank you to Matt Harmon, Simon Halliday, Martin Mills, and everyone at 4AD and Beggars Group around the world.

Thank you to the many friends, bandmates, colleagues, and readers who have helped me along the way, many of whom had roles in these stories: Danielle Fagre Arlowe, Jonah Bergman, Julie Butterfield, Scott Clampett, Eric Corson, Mike Davis, Ryann Donnelly, Dana Erickson, Steph Fairweather, Jasmine Faustino, Seth Fein, Jami Floyd, Tariq Goddard, Lisa Gottheil, Meghan Helsel, Jeff Hiatt, John Hodgman, Jessica Hopper, Jason Hughes, Chase Jarvis, Steve Kandell, Barbara Kass and Chris Kaufman, Blaise Allysen Kearsley, Jason Krevey, Sasha Laman, Jason Livermore, Greg Lovell, Shannon Luders-Manuel, Ray Mineau, Robby Morris, Sean Murray, Laura Neilson, Lance Paine, Tree Paine, Scott Parker, Jimmy Paulson, Joe Reineke, Don Robertson, John Roderick, Jonathan Rothman, Jeff Rouse, Brent Saunders, John Schiefer, Charles Sipos, Gabe Spierer, Mike Squires, Tommy Stinson, Jason Sutherland, Claire Taylor, Matt Vaughan, Mike Venutolo-Mantovani, Joe Wong.

Thank you to the artists whose music played in the background while this book took shape, including but not limited to Roy Ayers, Bad Brains, Patricia Brennan, Kate Bush, Alice Coltrane, Angel Bat Dawid, Kiss, Kraftwerk, Fela Kuti, Mtume Umoja Ensemble, Pixies, SAULT, and Stevie Wonder.

Thank you to the Brooklyn Historical Society for the wonderful library where much of this manuscript was written.

And thank you to Sarah Sloane, the college professor whose writing class I loved enough to earn an A.